THE MADNESS OF WAR

CHANNING KURY

TABLE OF CONTENTS

DEDICATION

FOR MY SONS, Matthew and Wendell, I dedicate this excursion into my elemental analysis of reality and life as it is lived with the hope that some pain may be avoided and more happiness achieved through a better understanding of the forces that shape our lives.

I also take this opportunity to pay homage to John Ferguson who, as an English instructor, attempted to instill psychological insight into Hamlet to students at The Mercersburg Academy, including myself, who read the drama but did not understand except in a nominal way the vectors in the human mind. When I complained sometime during the 1965-1966 school year that I was dreadfully bored and frustrated with the mandated English curriculum, he was kind enough to steer me to Robert Ardrey's African Genesis as alternative reading. I regret that I failed to keep in contact with him and he passed away in 2006. Although I have been influenced, befriended and guided by many instructors, John Ferguson was a gardener of lotus buds that with the passing seasons bloomed into Monet's Water Lilies. I thank John Ferguson for his kindness and generosity of spirit towards me as well as to others.

Many of the issues addressed in this discourse were raised by Prof. Lauriston Sharpe in his anthropology lectures at Cornell University, including the significance of the recurrence in many societies of tri-partite ("three") beliefs (he stated the query something along the lines of "three" as a magical or most significant number) and, as a separate query, whether Freudian philosophy is universal or culturally based (at least at that time the predominant belief seemed to be that Freudian thought was a Western European artifact). One Thursday afternoon in September, 1968, Prof. Sharpe and I had a brief private talk in which he suggested using an anthropological lens to analyze the then raging Viet Nam War. I do not think that we ever talked privately again but I must say that he suggested in that conversation and his lectures the intellectual viability of questions that might otherwise pass as trivial notions.

I also thank the late Al Utton at the University of New Mexico School of Law for his acts of kindness and friendship over many years. One such act was his green lighting the publication in the Natural Resources Journal of my essay Prolegomena to Conservation: a fisheye review.

HOW TO READ THE SYMPHONY OF THE MIND

I RECOMMEND THAT you read first all of the prefatory materials and all of the chapters in the order presented without reading the end notes. It may help if you consider *The Symphony of the Mind* as a puzzle rather than a traditional essay. Alternatively, consider yourself first unfolding an origami "white paper" exposition of philosophy and subsequently folding the white paper back into a model of the psyche.

Pause for a few days and then read all of end notes in sequence without going back to the main text. Many of the end notes are presented to clarify the otherwise terse text but some are mini-essays that can get you well on your way on a journey through a rabbit tunnel. For the time being, expand your understanding of the end notes by consulting other materials that you deem appropriate.

Pause once again for a few days. Return to the beginning and read *The Symphony of the Mind* through to the end of the primary text but this time read each of the end notes at the time you read the related passage in the primary text.

In doing so "Step by Step," you will achieve a mastery of the methodology that I am proposing to be centrally relevant to living one's life well.

A few questions that you might have after proceeding as I have suggested are addressed in "In Case You Wanted to Ask."

In a broad sense, this essay follows the law school "IRAC" model of Issue, Rule, Application and Conclusion. Here the issue is presented by the introduction with the rule being the model; application follows in the argument and the conclusion is presented in Q. E. D.

Somewhat like Robert M. Pirsig, I claim no expertise in either psychology or Zen Buddhism. The Symphony of the Mind, in the spirit of Zen and the Art of Motorcycle Maintenance, is a strange and twisted autobiography with many liberties taken with the facts as they may have occurred in life. The use of the term "autobiography" here is deliberate since *The Symphony of the Mind* is the product of my own introspection which created this map of my mind.

So let us, much like the White Rabbit in Lewis Carroll's *Alice's Adventures in Wonderland*, begin at the beginning and go on till we come to the end at which time we will stop.

PREFACES

FIRST PREFACE

Petites Madeleines

"MANY YEARS HAD elapsed during which nothing of Combray, save what was comprised in the theatre and the drama of my going to bed there, had any existence for me, when one day in winter, on my return home, my mother, seeing that I was cold, offered me some tea, a thing I did not ordinarily take. I declined at first, and then, for no particular reason, changed my mind. She sent for one of those squat, plump little cakes called 'petites madeleines,' which look as though they had been moulded in the fluted valve of a scallop shell. And soon, mechanically, dispirited after a dreary day with the prospect of a depressing morrow, I raised to my lips a spoonful of the tea in which I had soaked a morsel of the cake. No sooner had the warm liquid mixed with the crumbs touched my palate than a shudder ran through me and I stopped, intent upon the extraordinary thing that was happening to me. An exquisite pleasure had invaded my senses, something isolated, detached, with no suggestion of its origin. And at once the vicissitudes of life had become indifferent to me, its disasters innocuous, its brevity illusory — this new sensation having had on me the effect which love has of filling me with a precious essence; or rather this essence was not in me it was me. I had ceased now to feel mediocre, contingent, mortal. Whence could it have come to me, this all-powerful joy? I sensed that it was connected with the taste of the tea and the cake, but that it infinitely transcended those savors could not, indeed, be of the same nature. Whence did it come? What did it mean? How could I seize and apprehend it?"

Proust's "Petites Madeleines"

Balls and Strikes

THREE HOME PLATE umpires are at a bar drinking beer and discussing how they call balls and strikes in baseball games.

The first umpire says: "I call them as they are."

The second umpire then says: "No, no — I call them as I see them."

The third umpire takes a sip of beer, looks at the other two umpires, and says: "I don't know about you guys but until I call them they do not exist."

Sokol, pp. 52–53.

OM

"If the soul is an arrow and absolute truth the target, OM is the bow."

Rubin Museum, NYC
04/20/2017

FOURTH PREFACE

Memory and Observation

TRUTH EXISTS SOMEWHERE between memory and observation, with rules of its own that affect both the memory and the observation by which we interpret reality.

CK

FIFTH PREFACE

The Widening Gyre

"Turning and turning in the widening gyre

The falcon cannot hear the falconer;

Things fall apart; the centre cannot hold;

Mere anarchy is loosed upon the world;

The blood-dimmed tide is loosed, and everywhere

The ceremony of innocence is drowned;

The best lack all conviction, while the worst

Are full of passionate intensity."

W. B. Yeats, The Second Coming (1919).

SIXTH PREFACE

The Big Short

"WHILE THE WHOLE world was having a big ol' party, a few outsiders and weirdos saw what no one else could. … These outsiders saw the giant lie at the heart of the economy. And they saw by doing something the rest of the suckers never thought to do: they looked."

> The Big Short screenplay by
> Charles Randolph and Adam McKay
> (based upon the book by Michael Lewis)
> p. 5 (Buff Revised, May 11, 2015).

SEVENTH PREFACE

Adjournment

"When shall we three meet again?

In thunder, lightning or in rain?"

> The first of three Witches
> William Shakespeare,
> The Tragedy of Macbeth
> (Act 1, Scene 1).

INTRODUCTION

My dear Matti Bucca and Villi Boca,

This letter to you, now an expanded essay, began long before you were born, even before I met your mother. I was sitting in my apartment in San Francisco when, lacking anything better to do, I began an inquiry into the causes of war. This inquiry eventually focused on the query: "Why would fathers send their sons into a war that could not be won?"

This query arose in part out of the domestic turmoil in America during the Viet Nam War. America's excursion was doomed to failure and terrible costs were imposed on America as well as Viet Nam. What became evident during the course of the war was that what began as an exercise in geopolitics became warped by the psyches of America's leaders and the souls of American families. This Titanic struggle between power and love cannot be understood without a schematic understanding of the mind. To that end it is necessary to plumb the depths of the psyche to learn why we were in Viet Nam.

Introspection is difficult because life propels us beyond our comprehension as we must often act as best we can without the benefit of reasoning abilities and information sufficient to achieve a state of repose of the optimum optimorum. The mind in the guise of its psyche is a Gordian Knot whose solution is beyond the ken of ordinary discourse. One of the characteristics of a Gordian Knot is all of the fibers are hugely interwoven so that many connections are obscured or blocked from view. One notorious solution to the Gordian Knot riddle of antiquity was that by Alexander who cut the knot with a sword, an exercise of power. Power reaches conclusions without the benefits of understanding and resolution.

To understand the mind one needs to comprehend the mind as an entire system unto itself and then unweave the threads of thought. Sigmund Freud provided the instructions on how to do this deconstruction via his core concepts of the id, ego and superego. However, Freudian analysis is an extraordinarily arduous undertaking in large part due to Freudian Doctrine placing obstacles to reaching understanding.

The mind as a system unto itself is only partially verbal. We try to understand natural phenomena using words but the forces of nature act independent of whatever words we associate with them. So the mind creates reality that is partially independent of words. That phenomenon is perfected in the actor's craft as Stella Adler explained the imbuing of a character's psyche into an actor's performance in her lectures on master playwrights. Memorization of a script is not enough to enable an actor to perform. An actor needs to express the vectors that are within the playwright's language. A system of thought, a philosophy, is essential to the understanding of what would otherwise be a catalogue of information. The core function of a philosophy is the provision of mental vectors as keys to transition from one fact to the next.

My letter to you, converted by end notes into a book, addresses the conundrum of the relationship between the individual and society but my specific argument is for the rise of the individual as a self-actualizing reasonable adventurer who is free to be a conscientious objector to war and who is otherwise licensed to conduct civil disobedience so that, in the end, he is the master of his fate by the supremacy of his soul.

FREUDIAN DOCTRINE

Sigmund Freud solved the essence of the problem by introducing concepts of the forces that create our minds. In addition to his theory of the mind, he developed some useful tools such as the idea that a key to interpreting dreams is analyzing them as strivings for wish fulfillment.

Can one go to Freud's writings to solve real problems? That would be an awful lot of reading resulting in no definitive answers. See "The Probability of Truthful Statements," infra. As best as I can tell, Freud never completely synthesized his most developed conception of the human psyche. All of his writings were works in progress that, when cobbled together into a canon, created a working but not definitive map of the mind.

Some commentators like to argue that Freud was wrong about this or that with the commentator pointing to some statement Freud made in the course of his life. As a practical matter, those commentators are arguing with a dead man as a straw man. Freudian Doctrine does not exist except as the figment of a commentator's imagination or one's own over reliance on the manner by which Freud expressed his ideas. There are no absolute Freudian precepts for how to live one's life.

Freudian concepts have evolved and alternative formulations have become convenient translations. Prominent reformulations include Carl Jung's, which may be the most accessible. Analysts, whether medically trained or otherwise, are not monopolists of truth nor should they be gurus proclaiming truth.

But the problem still persists of doctrine as Freud's leftover baggage, those formulations in a time and place that no longer exist. Is it possible to reformulate Freudian theory into a modern tool of analysis not only of the human psyche but also social policy? I suggest that it can but not by some one-to-one corresponding algorithm. The idea is to convert the core dynamics of Freudian psychology into neutral principles of analysis notwithstanding that the vast majority of people do not believe, accept or utilize neutral principles. Thus, my argument for a general model of the mind in this Chautauqua talk will begin.

THE MODEL

IN DISCUSSING PHILOSOPHY, it is easy to conflate beliefs and models. Although I state many beliefs about many topics, my formulation of P-T-R elemental analysis is a model. I happen to believe that it is a powerful model that generates a vast array of useful information that individuals might not otherwise access. But one does not live by models but by beliefs. To the extent that beliefs can be more informed by models, life can be enhanced.

Freud was correct in his belief that the psyche has three elemental components: the id, ego and superego, which he discovered by inductive reasoning from direct observation. I propose to strip these concepts of their subjectivity, sexual connotations and Freud's baggage and denote the elements by the names Homo theatrica ("T"), Homo rationale ("R"), and Homo politico ("P"). The stripping of concepts to their skeletons turns the argument from inductive reasoning to deductive logic ala Euclid. This alternative method of explaining the psyche is "elemental analysis."

There are two very different types of logic: external and internal. External logic is the logic that is expressed in oral and written discourse, most rigorously and formally in mathematics but broadly speaking in scholastic philosophy. Internal logic is the logic of the mind. Elemental analysis is a description of internal logic. Stages of truth are evolving paradigms of understanding typically but not exclusively on a personal or individual basis.

There are three and only three primordial elements (T, R & P), which I will shortly define for you, from which the scaffolding of the universe of knowledge can be derived. But this discourse is not some abstract exercise. Philosophy is the stuff of life as the Balls and Strikes joke in the second preface illustrates the merger of thought and reality.

Each element is distinguished by a primary characteristic that corresponds to observable reality as identity (Homo theatrica), reason (Homo rationale) and power (Homo politico). These elements combine to create the constructs of thought and expression whether through language or action.

We start with observation that the mind, by necessity, is a unified system of thought. The mind must be able to communicate within itself. That process creates concepts that obey rules that organize the concepts so that the concepts emerge through the psyche as thought and action.

Thoughts and actions are observable and can be deconstructed. If the methodology actually corresponds in reverse order to the creation of a particular thought or action, then it may be said to be a true and useful map of the mind. How would one know if the methodology is in fact a reverse correspondence? The test is whether after many deconstructions there is a convergence of concepts. If there is no convergence, then my thesis fails; if there is convergence, then quod erat demonstrandum.

However, the general rule for P-T-R analysis is to apply the model and work outward towards meaning additional to what was already at hand. Reversing the order from meanings to model is a test of the model but does not normally generate additional meaning. Elemental analysis is a model that progressively builds upon itself. It is the reiteration of the method that generates the increasing scale and complexity of the analysis.

The basic premise is that all thought is composed of elements that obey rules of composition. The rules of composition apply not only to the internal communication within the mind but also to the perception of external phenomena. In other words, the rules provide the vehicle by which the imaginary universe of the mind translates the real universe of all phenomena external to the mind itself.

Each mind begins with nothing and builds an enormously complex model of itself and the universe. To answer the question "What is the first step?," it is helpful first to describe the simplest thoughts and then go back to the beginning.

Consider two postulates:

1. Every thought is composed of 3 elements and only 3 elements.
2. These elements are real and behave by rules of existence even though they otherwise only exist in the medium of a brain serving as the physical scaffolding of the mind.

To understand the P-T-R model, you must accept the originating assumptions and sequentially rigorously apply logic. When you reach an absurdity, apply the model to the absurdity, treating the absurdity as an original proposition.

THE THREE ELEMENTS

The three elements are:

P which is a "greater than / lesser than" function.

T which is an "equal to" function.

R which is a readjustment function (mediation).

The P element corresponds with Freud's concept of the super-ego. The "P" reformulation may be referenced to an archetype denominated Homo politico.

The T element corresponds with Freud's concept of the id. The "T" reformulation may be referenced to an archetype denominated Homo theatrica.

The R element corresponds with Freud's concept of the ego. The "R" reformulation may be referenced to an archetype denominated Homo rationale. Logic or reason is a lemma that reconciles power and image to achieve some stage of truth.

The elements of statements create the Freudian mind (and not vice versa) and the three faces of one's soul that is trapped inside the Gordian Knot of the mind. Unraveling and teasing out the knot's strands is a method for decoding the mind's messages to you. You can not be rational if you do not know the boundaries of your analysis. Analysis of the boundaries is also necessary. Having done that, then you need to venture beyond the pale and survey the outer terrain. Conventional "rational" analysis is a conservative, identity limiting, approach to living one's life. It over assesses risks and under estimates long term gains. Short run (term) rationality is not necessarily congruent with long run (term) rationality and optimality.

PRE- AND POST-PARTUM MIND

Freud's schema (id, superego and ego or any other order you prefer) describes the psychological development of a child after the child's birth. But, the child's mind has already at birth by necessity developed a structure that allows it to interpret or translate perceptions. While the child was in utero, the child's universe was defined by the mother's body and what few external events that reached the fetus (e.g., sounds, pressure, medical devices, fluctuations in sugar and nutrients).

PRE-PARTUM MIND

The creation of a child's mind begins in the physics and chemistry of the emerging brain. At some point in the early development of the fetus, an elixir of mind is present but blank. This elixir has the special characteristic of translating perception into an abstract structure that is readable by the child's brain. (This phenomenon is consciousness which is considered to be a "big question" in science that eludes explication.)

The elixir is some form of electro-chemical soup. This soup has the characteristic of receiving an initial stimulus and then organizing its structure into any of three alternative forms. There may be some law of physics as to the nature of matter itself that could come into play at this moment in the development of the fetal brain. Until the first stimulus, the elixir can not think and is otherwise incapable of processing information. Its composition is such that an electro-chemical code can be created out of building blocks that by themselves cannot function as mental forces. The initial stimulus forces the elixir to choose to organize itself and, thereby, creates the template for the cusp of personality for a fetus.

A stimulus, a precipitating event, is capable of creating a template for organizing mental processes, development and behavior. An example is the phenomenon of imprinting noted by Douglas Spalding, advanced by Oskar Heinroth and famously demonstrated by Konrad Lorenz. Lorenz separated incubated goose eggs into groups and arranged, that upon hatching, that the goslings in different sets would initially observe different large moving objects. Some saw a goose and thereafter followed that goose as their mother. Others saw Lorenz and followed him.

Thought does not exist in some abstract ether. It is created by a bio-chemical process in the evolution of species and, in particular, Homo sapiens. The genetic component came out of Darwinian natural selection. By a fortuitous genetic event, Homo sapiens was endowed with a set of genes that create the bio-chemical "soup" that organizes itself into the cusp of personality. Other species, such as the cetaceans and ravens, had their own similar fortuitous genetic events; similar not identical. Their fundamental coding creates different bio-chemical soups which develop into the peculiar intelligence idiosyncratic to each of the intelligent species, which is why their logics are different and, thus, while we can signal messages to other species and partially decode their languages, we can never truly converse with them.

Query: Could a structure of knowledge be based on the sense of smell or taste or touch? I believe that a creature totally lacking sight and hearing could create a complex corpus of knowledge based on the sense of smell or taste or touch but it would need, what otherwise might not be present, a genetic code that allows the reorganization of thought within the creature's nervous system. A relevant obiter dictum is Bernard B. Fall's noting that: ""All the stenches of nature seemed to be on the loose. There are layers of odors, slices of odors, packages of odors, odors for my nose and for everyone else's in the world. Too bad that there isn't yet a standard system to translate odors into colors. If one could translate those stenches into colors Picasso's wildest abstractions would look like a painting by Grandma Moses." Bernard B. Fall, Street Without Joy p. 112. Sight or hearing are themselves insufficient to create the higher intelligence. Using reverse logic, this observation seems to imply that higher thought or intelligence can exist based on other sensory inputs.

As a gedanken, a thought experiment, query if Homo sapiens were ever to have contact with intelligent extraterrestrial life ("E-T"), would we be able to converse with E-T beings? Even if the E-T beings were to have a P-T-R structure for thought and speech, the E-T language would undoubtedly be in a form incomprehensible to us, much as the languages of cetaceans are largely beyond our ken. The approach to take would be the deciphering the language as a code with an internal logic. Once the form of the internal logic is discovered and an external reference point (if you prefer, a Rosetta Stone) that corresponds to a fragment of the language is found, then a translation could be built.

A one-to-one correspondence is not necessarily a simple straightforward process. The complexity of correspondence was demonstrated regarding music copyright at the continuing legal education program "Scales of Justice" (NYC May 23, 2012). This performance's ramifications went well beyond technical issues of equivalence in music notation and copyright law for the program addressed fundamentals such as recognition, knowledge and belief.

As a query implicit in the E-T language query, consider whether true intelligence can ever be in a form other than P-T-R. There are many logics executable by machines. The classic (but fallible) test of whether computers have "intelligence" is that proposed by Alan Turing in testing whether "Can machines think?" by determining whether communications between a machine and a human are indistinguishable by a human evaluator. If the evaluator can not determine which half of the conversation comes from which entity, then the machine passes the Turing Test.

Crossing over to animal life forms, insects (even honey bees and ants) and reptiles are biological robots. Elements of true intelligence are present in some birds (such as ravens and parrots) and complex thought seem to be present in many mammals (such as apes, cetaceans, maybe elephants). Human intelligence evolved from an evolutionary ancestor shared with, at least, the apes. One would suspect that the highly intelligent mammals share in their respective ontogenies some rudimentary P-T-R structure that in Homo sapiens becomes, through some genetic device, more enriched with R than other mammals. Thus, one can argue, in regards to extra-terrestrial life created by alternative biological chemistry, that P-T-R is sui generis to earth's Homo sapiens.

On earth, a benchmark in the rise of intelligence from 66 million years ago is the K-T [K-Pg] boundary that marks the demise of dinosaurs and emergence of mammals as a dominant life form. Birds being descendants of dinosaurs can arguably have an independent source of enriched R in their mental processes, separate from the progressive enrichment of R in mammals. Although a common ancestral source is conceivable, it is not surprising that R enrichment could have arisen in multiple independent events (including those enrichments that died out in extinct lines) because, in order for the mental processes to function at all, the core bioelectric "liquid crystal" must have the same or analogous skeletal structure. The evolution of mammals over the course of 63 million years or so led to the major enrichment of R to appear in man about 3 million years ago followed by both biophysical and cultural evolution which continues to this day although I find it convenient to use the last Ice Age of 10,000 years ago as a marker but not a cause of modern man.

STAGES OF PRE-CONSCIOUS DEVELOPMENT

The period of time from the zygote through the ectoderm's neural plate development is about 16 days. The second stage (which takes about 30 days) is that of neural fluid and tissue forming a neural tube which closes at about 46 days, which is followed by the partition of the emerging brain tissue into development of neural structures and a neural network. The originating organization of the cusp of personality through the sense of touch occurs at about 56 days. Thus, the die is cast and a sentient life's great adventure begins.

If my assumption that an external stimulus is the force that precipitates the creation of the cusp of personality, then the event would occur about this date (development age of 56 days) in development or perhaps a few days later. If the originating stimulus is not external but endogenous, then of course the initial formation of the seed cusp of personality could occur earlier. If the organizing force is not endogenous but an external stimulus, the most likely candidate from the five senses (touch, taste, smell, sight and hearing) would almost have to be touch as touch is believed to be the first of the sensory systems to function in an embryo.

Reality and truth do not exist in the absence of an organizing event or principle, or until they are organized by an event or principle. An analogy in chemistry is a supersaturated solution which does not crystalize until the insertion of a seed crystal or the existence of an imperfection in the otherwise perfectly smooth interior of its container. An analogy in physics is Schrodinger's Cat. In pure mathematics, the proof is Godel's Theorem.

The key to consciousness is the ability to talk, to communicate beyond mere signaling. Interpersonal talking must correspond to the mind's internal reasoning (its own intrapersonal talking), otherwise the interpersonal talking could not occur. It seems then to be possible to decode the inner mind by deconstructing its expressions through an analytical technique of deconstructing by retrogression. Graham Coleman, an editor of The Tibetan Book of the Dead (The Great Liberation by Hearing in the Intermediate States), suggests that "our text can then be seen as providing a guide for tracing our confused and deluded states, back through our conditioned attraction and aversion to selected aspects of our experience, back through the weave of our habitual tendencies and mental constructs and a relentless series of voluntary or involuntary mental choices, back through the illusory comfort generated by our sense of ego, right back to a pure original cognitive event."

Not only is there a correspondence, but there is parallelism, i.e., the logic at each level is parallel to each of the other levels. Corresponding sets are not necessarily parallel. The P-T-R model specifies that the entire series of sets of P-T-R structures has correspondence and parallelism.

An overly simplistic analogy can illustrate the point. Radio transmitters and receivers must be tuned to the same wavelength for substantive communication to occur. If out of synch, the receiver could detect the existence of a transmitter and could interpret some information by the timing and length of the static but we would not learn much more than we do when we listen to mockingbirds sing.

RATE OF GROWTH OF INTELLIGENCE

We know that the rate of growth of intelligence is extraordinary rapid because we know the length of time is takes from the initiating event (the seed of intelligence) to the fruition of fully functioning intelligence in an individual. If we could measure the number of units of intelligence of a fully functioning individual, we could mathematically model the growth from the first unit with three elements to the target number of units over the time of ontogeny as well as being able to calculate the amount of time it takes to create one unit of intelligence.

On the assumption that my model is correct, the mathematical scaffolding would be something like:

x = units of intelligence.

y = number of elements (which is always three times the number of units of intelligence).

t = time interval in which a new unit of intelligence is created. (The actual time unit is assumed to be constant.)

n = the number of elapsed time intervals after the creation of the first unit (i.e., the age of the individual measured by the number of time units [t] in which subsequent new units of intelligence are created which would not necessarily be the same as the amount of time needed to create the first [template] unit).

A value table would start at 2 rather than one because the time interval between 0 and 1 (creation of the template) is not necessarily the constant for replicating the template. The first step in replication is the step from 1 (the template) to 2 (creation of the first unit of intelligence from the template created in step 1); thus, the first step in a value table would be denominated 2 as being the first step of the progression after creating the template in step 1.

I guess that in twelve steps a half million units of intelligence with one-and-a-half million interfaces are created. Eventually, this model would progressively deviate from the actual rate of accumulation of units of intelligence as the percentage of units that multiple progressively drop from close to 100% toward a lesser percentage that represents the rate needed for mental maintenance. This point in humans occurs at about the age of 25 or 26 years, which is the age of maximum intelligence in humans. I believe that this is the tipping point for the mind which up to this age is busy acquiring models of thought but then works with what it has for the life tasks that arise. Basically, the mind shifts its focus from the R intensive model construction of why (development of competency) to P - T template instructions of how (encyclopedia of methods).

A more complete model would generate a sigmoid curve that reflects the progressive change from maximum growth to maintenance. This model does not address the eventual questions about the eventual decline in intelligence but my guess that senility arises from the deterioration of the organic brain which reduces the brain's capacity to support consciousness and other mental functions.

As we grow older, our sense of smell and taste changes (they might become more "educated"), a certain amount of the change can be ascribed to physiology but the major portion results, as adults, from the ongoing developing mind (not the brain except as diseases of senility set in). Similarly, the interpretation of touch also changes. The relationship between physiology and psychology re smell, taste and touch is complexly intertwined but the mind is the ultimate arbitrator of meaning.

The ultimate cause of "natural death" is the mind's decision to progressively shut down the host's human corpus, typically initially from the extremities then progressively to the body's organs. One implication of the P-T-R model is that aging, aside from physiological disease, can be delayed or diminished by diverse stimulation of the mind. A key concept is that the mind decides at some point that it is time for the body to die. In an overly simplified way, I am arguing that the decision to die is a product of the inadequate stimulation of diverse portions of the brain-mind duplex. The initiating decision is made long before the process can be detected. In essence, the mind decides that it is time to die when the balance and degree (magnitude) of stimuli are so deficient that the mind in a multitudinous series of tiny stages weans the corpus from continuing support. Eventually, the lack of support cascades and the remaining systems shut down.

Which gets us back to the role of naturalists who can directly observe the phenomenon of the brain and mind. Someone will eventually measure the units of intelligence in a person or the rate of creation of units of intelligence and will thereby validate or refute this model. As an observer of nature, I, like many other naturalists, continue to be amazed and surprised at what we learn as we continue watching. The natural world is full of surprises and these surprises provide the bridges across our chasms of ignorance.

There is an observation that suggests that the time interval for creating a unit of intelligence is a tenth of a second or less. That observation is based on the "missing moment" where memory is not formed if the memory process is disturbed. It takes one-tenth of a second for the mind to memorialize sensory inputs. If the process is disrupted, no memory is created and as a consequence, of course, the event cannot be recalled. In a sense, the mind is always a tenth of a second behind the external world and, thus, can never be in perfect synchronization with external events. See Robert Pollack's The Missing Moment: how the unconscious shapes modern science (1999). If that observation corresponds with the creation of one intelligence unit (and the resulting elemental interfaces), then it is possible to estimate the size of the brain-mind complex at different stages of ontogeny and compare those estimates with the capacity that a computer would need to do those corresponding life stage tasks.

The mind has an internal biological clock (an endogenous self sustaining oscillator), the speed and period of which may vary among individuals. In contrast to the hormone driven physiological clocks of animals which are set by outside events (typically by first light and the length of daylight), humans have the ability to set, read and manage their internal clocks. People can decide to wake up from a night's sleep earlier than their normal waking and without the benefit of an external alarm by deliberately deciding the evening before that they will wake up at, say, 4:00 a.m. The actual waking process is physiological but the mental processes of the mind uses an abstract concept, to wit: "4:00 a.m.", to change or manage the physiology of waking. Thus, the mind can read its own internal clock.

There are other time characteristics of the mind. A fundamentally important example is that reflexes, which take place in about one-hundredth of a second, are faster than consciousness. You may remember a reflexive action but your memory took longer to form than the reflex action itself to occur. To wit: you can remember the occurrence but not while it is taking place. Life is faster than our ability to instantaneously analyze what is happening. Which raises the question of when to parse or not to parse? To live in the moment? Joy or regret? Galen Strawson's discussion of the variance between substantial and precise recollection can be parsed on the basis that the mind, being the repository of memory, uses its own structure to encode the discussion or event in contrast with other persons' own memory encoding or, for that matter, the mechanical recording, whether video, audio, or other, of the discussion or event. Because of differences in the encoding, variations in memory are inevitable. See Galen Strawson, Things That Bother Me: death, freedom, the self, etc. (2018) p. 65.

For my entire life, I have had a problem of remembering the names of people that I just met. An inept Freudian explanation would be something like I was repressing a name because the person in some manner reminded me of an unpleasant person or event. While that may have been true in a few particular cases, a better explanation is that, during the moment (about one-tenth of a second) that my mind needed to process the memorialization of a name, my mind interrupted that process because it was attempting to process what I was about to say to that person.

Since I am discussing the timing mechanism of the mind via the brain's processing of information, I should mention that a suggestion has been made that the "conscious now", alternatively the "ego", exists within a time frame of about three seconds. See Strawson, supra p. 42 and footnotes at p. 219.

If the three seconds ego is valid, then it may be the measurement of the time it takes the mind to rotate through or cycle through one loop. It would follow then that a sequence of thought is composed bits of three seconds, which may be the basis for the length of time for a complete thought process. Twenty bits in a minute leads to a thousand bits in a fifty minute hour, which may be of some meaning to practicing psychoanalysts.

Query: Is there any significance to a kilobit chain of thought? Is there some dynamic in the mind that normal sustained thought runs its course minutes short of an hour? Of course, thought can be fleeting or prolonged but what insight can be gained by examining this commonly recurring time frame? Consider that classroom lectures and many television programs are approximately 50 minutes long. Psychiatric therapy sessions have traditionally been scheduled on the basis of a "Fifty Minute Hour." See, e.g., Robert M. Lindner, The Fifty-Minute Hour (1955). Mere coincidence? Product of extraneous factors?

An ultimate, perhaps unattainable, goal is a mind with its elements (P, T & R) coordinated among themselves in synchrony with the mind's endogenous self-sustaining oscillator (its "biological clock"). One then has a sense of control of one's life, a mastery of one's destiny. The mind's biological clock is the conductor of of the symphony of the mind and is a portal to reality, the means by which we reference our souls with our environments. The characteristics of the clock are well known. For example, individual clocks are endogenously out of phase with the physical world and are reset by external stimuli such as light. The meshing or clashing of one's sense of time with other persons' senses of time as well as with the various cycles in diverse physical environments is a fundamental problem in how to live well.

CARTESIAN GRAPHING OF THE ACCUMULATION OF ICONS

Quadrant I

x = events in time sequence (Time is ambiguous in the absence of events; events mark time. An event is a stimulus that creates an icon.)

y = number of icons (Icons are items upon which meaning is projected; symbols are externally created to represent something.) The maximum value for y represents the total reservoir of knowledge for an individual.

y = x to the third power (which generates a very steep curve of the combinations and permutations of icons approaching or almost becoming a vertical line that projected onto the x axis generates an x value that represents the outer limit of intelligence and knowledge. The x value is at least 3 for most "higher" animals but I guess for humans is somewhere in the range of 10 to 20 and x corresponds to "intelligence" or IQ. The area between the y axis and the curve represents the applicable knowledge within the ambit of the individual, perhaps construable as "working knowledge."

DISTRIBUTION OF P–T–R PERMUTATIONS

I have assumed that the smallest possible seed crystal for abstract thought is composed of three elements in a structure that is shaped or configured by how the elements can interface with each other. I concede that alternative seed structures might be the basis of thought. A hollow sphere or other structure with an interactive surface or even some characteristic of an electro-chemical soup might be the seed.

Working on the assumption that the seed crystal is composed of the three elements, a distinguishing characteristic of the different seeds would be the order of bonding of the constituent elements.

P1-T2-R3 is not P1-R2-T3.

T1-P2-R3 is not T1-R2-P3.

R1-T2-P3 is not R1-P2-T3.

These combinations constitute a class of six seeds or archetypes. These seeds and their progeny have a range and probability of occurrence that approximates the range and probability of occurrence of human personality types. Perhaps the six most basic seeds are Jungian "archetypes."

The distribution of the seeds or archetypes can be graphed with the three axes of P, T and R in a three dimensional grid.

If one were able to measure the proportions of P, T and R in personalities, a datum could be placed on the grid. With a sufficient population (sample size) of data, the following characteristics of thought and personality could be graphed:

1. Range between the extreme limits

2. Probability (frequency) of occurrence of any particular P-T-R permutation (graphed along the Z axis of three dimensional Cartesian space)

3. The density within the range

4. The continuity or breaks within the range

5. The consistency (whether smooth or lumpy) of density within the range.

These characteristics could be graphed using the Z axis in the three dimensional Cartesian model. The resulting graph (being a side view of the graph otherwise viewed from above) could show a "bell shaped" normal probability distribution curve that is continuous and smooth tapering off at the extremes and the maximum value located somewhere between the extremes. Or, perhaps, the resulting graph would undulate through its range and possibly even have gaps or even have no major value curve. There are profound implications resulting from which, if either, Cartesian model is true. If the better model is not a smooth continuous bell shaped curve, then all deviations from a normal distribution and all gaps therein are pregnant with meaning.

BUILDING BLOCKS

P, T and R are true elements, analogous to atoms in chemistry. Think of building blocks that not just exist together in a structure but also dynamically interact with each other. Existing together is a diamond set in a ring; dynamic interaction is the courtship flight of a woodcock on an April evening. What are the laws of nature that modulate the interaction of these elements? Just what are these elements and from where did they spring into existence? That last question may be the fundamental question of the natural sciences. So why don't we go there to find the spark of intellect that will emerge at birth and develop into the raging fires of adolescence and adulthood.

The spark, the spark. How can we find the spark that starts it all? Well, we know that it does not exist prior to conception. The spark is not some free existing virus that enters an embryo ala deus ex machina to organize the chaotic emptiness of the developing mind.

The spark is struck by characteristics of the neural soup of biochemical compounds early in the gestation of the developing fetus, perhaps as early as the neural tube. These biochemical compounds, whatever the chemical properties that lead to their creation, at some point begin to interact with each other and create structures as products of the compounds' characteristics. An analogous process is the information created and preserved by the complementary chemical compounds of the double helix of DNA (Deoxyribo Nucleic Acid) which is composed of two inter-twining polymers fitted together with complementary pairs of the nucleo-tides: cytosine, adenine, guanine and thymine. However, DNA works at the molecular level but the P-T-R element structure is not composed of mole-cules themselves.

I do not know the biochemical formulas for the biochemical soup that create the elements P, T and R. That inquiry is well outside my skill set but I am confident that such compounds exist if for no other reason that there is no other means of creating a mind. I conjecture that the size of a loop by which reasoning occurs is smaller than a hydrogen atom but most certainly is not contained within atoms or free standing molecules. Rather the loops are either surface phenomena of matrixes of molecules or elec-tro-dynamic phenomena of some fluid structure of ions suspended in a cerebral fluid or gel or are suspended in a field or matrix between mole-cules. These possibilities seem to provide a basis for the geometry of a sta-ble and extensive network.

Let me leap over that chasm of ignorance and assume that it is true that there are biochemical compounds that create the elements P, T and R as characteristics of those compounds in situ. If that assumption is true, how do these elements interact and intellect emerge?

I postulate the following characteristics of P, T and R:

The building blocks are:

P   a "greater than / lesser than" function that is directional (to wit: can go in either of two directions but not both directions).

T   an equal function that goes in both directions simultaneously.

R   a compiler function that measures the strength of the P and T functions.

The electronic engineering model is important as the key to the internalization of the initial outside stimulus. The stimulus itself is not incorporated into the elixir. The elixir converts the disturbance into a P or T function in the electro-chemical soup. Every one of these concepts is ordinary and well within the ken of millions of engineers who can build numerous devices based on these concepts, but not a single one of those devices will have a psyche, cognition beyond computation. One could argue, since engineering is preeminently the understanding of systems, that the solution to the consciousness query will be found by an engineer.

Where is the magical transformation? Once the soup is organized into its most rudimentary structure, it is no longer soup but is now a pro-to-mind. The rules by which the proto-mind then developes are no longer electro-chemical engineering rules. The developmental rules exist and are testable.

What is this logic of the internal mind? Possible candidates include a single premise ("There exist a point") and any number of binary logics. These candidate systems operate in a universe of rationality but we know that life is irrational. Life is explicable if, when we look into the pit's mouth, we see a Tertium Quid. Freud's trip-partite model is the foundation for creating a model that not only explains but also analyses in neutral terms that which may be subjective and idiosyncratic.

Rather than outlining and otherwise discussing Freud's concepts of the superego, id and ego, I will take the unconventional step of ignoring the task of establishing any one-to-one correspondence between Freud's concepts and my elements of Homo politico, Homo theatrica and Homo rationale, which for convenience I denote as P, T and R. I assume that the correspondence exists but I will leave the academic task of that particular validation to others who may be so inclined.

PATH OF MENTAL DEVELOPMENT
AND THE MOBIUS STRIP CONJECTURE

The path of mental development is constrained by the parallel development of the brain from an elixir micro-drop through neural tube to segmented brain. The mind exists; it is real; and it resides in the brain. The
shape of the mind develops from the early bundle of Mobius loops to a
network congruently shaped with the physical landscape of the active portions of the brain. The consensus among neurologists is that the human
brain continues to develop as a bio-physical structure until about the age of
25. The distinction noted here is that large portions of the brain are struc-
turally and chemically supportive of the active portion. Thus, it is incorrect
to say that the mind is co-extensive with the gross brain. The mind and the
active brain are supported by the rest of the brain like the brain is supported nutritionally by the digestive system of the entire body.

Consider multitudes of Mobius loops that are running past each
other, each loop being attached at least temporarily to a multitude of other
loops which are also "running" and exchanging information. Information
("knowledge") is encoded in the P-T-R sequence on each Mobius strip.

Query: What are the width, thickness, length and speed of cycling
for the strips? As I mentioned earlier in "Building Blocks," I conjecture that
the size of a loop is smaller than a hydrogen atom but most certainly is not
contained within atoms. Rather the loops are either surface phenomena of
matrixes of molecules or electro-dynamic phenomena of some fluid structure of ions suspended in a cerebral fluid or gel or are suspended in a field
or matrix between molecules that might provide the geometry for a stable
and extensive network.

Why are the loops Mobius strips that run past each other and
exchange information at the parts of contact between different loops?
Reading either side of a Mobius surface gives you identical information,
which is not true of an ordinary loop with two surfaces. The argument that
a two sided (an ordinary "non-Mobius") band corresponds to duality in

the psyche, while initially superficially appealing, fails on the most unlikely one-to-one correspondence between the sides in the mechanical construction of the loop. A two sided loop would probably not be identical on both sides due to the structure of the loop itself. Thus, the encoded information would be different and interacting loops would read different messages depending on which side they are reading. As a Mobius strip rotate through its cycle any interacting loop would receive identical information.

PINPOINTS OF KNOWLEDGE THAT EXPLODE

Each loop is a Mobius strip that is continuously cycling while in contact with other Mobius strips. Three strips (inside, median and outside) share the same information from the median Mobius strip. Each of the strips has multiple corresponding pairs and, thereby, an exponential web of knowledge is created.

The Mobius strip is essential to a tri-partite model of the mind because only then do the inside strip and the outside strip read the same information from the median strip. (The assumption being that the strip has a thickness or structure so that the strip is not symmetrical and so that it is not identical on both sides at each point along the length of the strip.) Otherwise, if the strip is a two-sided loop, there would be no unification of the encoding point of knowledge. Mobius strips allow the tri-partite mind to have "multiple reads" of the same information.

An icon, perhaps in the form of a fractal, is a unit of translation and transference in the rotation of the loops. If three combined entities (a triad) have in fact the smallest amount of information to create a pattern (an icon), then omne trium perfectum. When an equivalence or a correspondence occurs, the thought process moves from one loop to the next loop. The thought continues through the rotation of that loop until another different correspondence with another loop occurs. At that point, the thought process moves to this third loop and would continue to work its way through the fourth, fifth, sixth, et seq. loops. A loop contains information that is in the form of a "repeatable narrative," i.e., every time the loop rotates through its cycle the narrative is the same. The message changes only when there is a loop transference.

Icons are riddles and are also portals through which we can be mentally transported in the form of illusions to another time, place and event. As you walk your path through life, you will encounter in your peregrinations, as you have already encountered, icons at every step. How you interpret these icons will determine the course of your life. So, come walk with me for awhile so I may give you some guidance in the interpretation of icons.

Consistent loops run continuously and ordinary events and thoughts are forgotten because they are consistent. But when an inconsistency occurs in the running of the loops, the loops pause and psychic pain erupts from the lack of power to resolve the inconsistency.

In running a loop, there may be non-functioning sections, perhaps 50% of the length of the band. A non-functioning section may be where the "switch" between loops occurs.

How many twists in the Mobius loop? I believe just one but Nature contains many surprises. There could be multiple twists in the "one-sided band." Query whether the speed of the loop's rotation is affected by the number of twists in the band? The speed of rotation is a critical factor in order that the processing can be completed for thoughts to emerge in real time. Query further whether more than one twist would cause the loop to kink?

These loops chain us to our pasts and in the present keep us in human bondage to forces that we may not want and can barely recollect. A more phantasmagorical image would be a complex of many carousels (merry-go-rounds) and a multitude of Ferris wheels that are interlocked by automatic transfer stations. These transfer stations are where metaphors work their magic in allowing you to see one thing as something else. Once you get on, you ride the circuit. Classical psychoanalysis involves the revisiting by verbally re-riding as many of the carousels and Ferris wheels of one's mind as is feasible. Unsatisfactory dreams that revisit earlier life events are like getting rides on carousels and Ferris wheels; you wake up and you are where you got on.

In mapping out your trip through a series of carousels and Ferris wheels, you are describing a path through the Gordian Knot of your mind. One way of visualizing this ride through your psyche is to imagine that you have teased out of such a knot a thread that you have stretched out over a time line. These threads are composed of bits (of about three seconds) that constitute, when strung together, the thought process (which of course may have various lengths). Recovery of ancient memory is also teasing out the cords then fibers of a Gordian knot, to wit: the moving from a current set of loops via a progression of intermediary loops to the functional memory of an ancient set of skills such as the gear shift pattern and clutching in a 1986 Tercel station wagon.

An alternative model is a fisheye lens kaleidoscope in which each fractal is another kaleidoscope containing fractals, each of which is a kaleidoscope containing kaleidoscopic fractals, et al. The fisheye lens is a physical metaphor for the curve of knowledge and the phenomena of expanding, exploding points of vision. For a verbal illustration of an "exploding point," see Proust's "Petites Madeleines" (First Preface, supra).

The curve of knowledge exists in many forms. If you are intrigued by the fisheye lens metaphor, consider:

1. kaleidoscopic fractals rotating in time and

2. the degree of perception and understanding are reduced as one looks through a fisheye lens from the center to the edge.

I argue that there is a curve in perception analogous to the curve in a photograph generated by a fisheye lens. This curve of perception and knowledge is not merely subjective and is not easily remedied by additional effort. The curve is a product of reality. Two examples come to mind.

In a well designed and well executed model of statistical probability, there is the phenomenon that a large population can have its characteristics accurately estimated by a sample of rather modest size. Obviously, accuracy increases as the sample size increases from 1 to some number that is a function of the population but the contribution to accuracy contributed by each additional unit at some point begins to diminish so that you reach a point where you will have an insignificant increase in accuracy even though you have, say at that point, doubled the sample size.

A second example is derived from trigonometry and calculus in perceiving a sphere such as a ball or the earth's moon from a distance. It is true that you can see an entire hemisphere but, even though you can detect characteristics to the edge of the hemisphere, the quality of perception decreases from the middle region of the hemisphere to the hemisphere's edge.

Michael Lewis made an observation in his The Big Short (2010) at p. 116 that seems to correspond with my argument that there is a curve in knowledge as an inherent characteristic of knowledge itself. "The model used by Wall Street to price trillions of dollars' [sic] worth of derivatives thought of the financial world as an orderly, continuous process. But the world was not continuous; it changed discontinuously, and often by accident." It is fundamental to his observation that, unlike the physical realities of the planet Jupiter, financial markets are created by thought. Years ago, before computers, the now defunct ticker tape machine reported the conclusions of many "thoughts." "Financial markets are a collection of arguments." Michael Lewis, The Big Short (2010), p. 79. Arguments are analyzable in terms of P-T-R and an entire market can be modeled using the P-T-R scaffolding and algorithms.

At the core of all sophisticated methodologies, regardless of their facial subjects, are simple, rather ordinary algorithms. The trick is know which of the myriad possible "simple algorithms" is at the core of any one methodology in order for that model to work in the real world of its subject matter (financial markets, sports betting, et al.) Investors become fools when they want to believe what they in fact do not understand, which is the classic case of taking a partial algorithm and acting on it as if it were comprehensive and all encompassing. It is not that a partial algorithm can not work; rather, to employ it in a meaningful manner requires time, energy and money or resources for implementation through the incorporation of additional algorithms. The most efficient strategy is to identify the core algorithm and work outward.

The faults in our thinking and the resulting errors in our actions are the entrances to the labyrinth of our minds. To live one's life on the basis of short term or near horizon rational decision making (treating life as a straight line process) leads to a very conservative (risk adverse) lifestyle that assumes away the discontinuities, the curve, inherent in life. Long term or far horizon decision making has a calculus that anticipates risk and accommodates change.

Boundaries between two sets of data can be consider a line of points and, if you can deconstruct a point, you can deconstruct a boundary line. This proposition is not just theoretical but has real world applications such as in disputes between adjoining landowners.

As a simple heuristic exercise, consider the question of "who gets the penny?" You are tasked with dividing, as a one time event, a sum of money equally between two persons. However, the sum to be divided includes an uneven number of cents. It is required that all of the money be distributed. Who gets the penny? There are many versions of this exercise. One example is that of two lawyers splitting 50/50 a $33,333.33 fee. Which one gets $16,666.66 and which one gets $16,666.67? Why? What is the rationale? The general problem is that of interpreting an event that is precisely within or on the boundary between two exclusive sets.

This simplest of examples is simply a demonstration that a point of knowledge, a tiny datum, can explode into entire realms of meaning.

PRE–PARTUM PERSONALITY

The pre-partum personality is determined by the P-T-R structure of the fetus' mind. By the time of birth, the mind has become a Gordian Knot of circuits in which there are preferred paths that were created in its development. The preference of certain paths over other paths is what gives the child its initial personality. This initial psyche is the infant's set of mental tools with which to explore life. In one sense, the first ethnic language that a child learns in infancy is a second language, the first language being the fetus' in utero thought language. Since the in utero thought language is the scaffolding for the learning of post-partum verbal language, the meaning of post-partum verbal communications is partially determined even before verbal language training begins.

Although the cusp of personality is stable and consistent throughout life, additional personality traits, components and compulsions are added as one develops, picking up facets (negative as well as positive) from interacting with and observing other people, including those who may no longer be physically in your life any more but who continue to live in your mind. Dual or even multiple originating icons may compete in the present.

As an example, my father smoked cigars and I, for a while as a young man, smoked and enjoyed smoking cigars. However, a series of conflicts with other people, as well as my understanding the health risks in continuing to smoke cigars, led me to cease smoking cigars even on rare occasions. From time to time, perhaps induced by a whiff of cigar smoke, I am tempted to find a great cigar and smoke it but I never do.

POST-PARTUM PERSONALITY

Beginning as an infant, all of us face a bewildering deluge of stimuli and information. How one reacts early on determines what set of tools one uses to work through infancy and adolescence. At least some of the compulsions exercised in later life are simply a continuation of an infant adopting an icon as a solution to a facet of the distress of being overwhelmed.

The initial birth personality is molded thereafter by interacting with the external world; Freudian factors progressively advance through childhood, puberty and adolescence; thereafter, the psyche deals with life with what tools it has at hand.

The concept of reincarnation of a person from a prior life into a present life is an artifact of the initial formulation of the cusp of personality, as being a characteristic of the personality that is not the product of training, conditioning or education. The XIVth Dalai Lama suggests that: "…the characteristics carried forward from a previous life are generally thought to be most strongly felt at an early stage of one's rebirth. This is because the personal characteristics of the previous life are thought, generally speaking, to be quickly overwhelmed by the developing characteristics inherited from the parents of the present life."

Progression in the ongoing development of the mind does not imply that the progression necessarily approaches an enhancement in rationality and balance; the progression can just as well lead to the intractability of the solidification of one's initial inclinations. Compulsions are attempts to rebalance the balance of power cast by pre-adolescent events.

There are well known stages of infant play (unoccupied play, solitary play, onlooker play, parallel play, associative play, cooperative play) that correspond with the growth and development of the P-T-R structure of the infant's mind. The stage of parallel play is particularly intriguing as the model for adults "talking past each other," i.e., having a conversation without engagement. Query whether many adults have ever progressed beyond associative play to cooperative play. Do adults yo-yo between the infant development stages? Perhaps acting momentarily in one stage but reverting to another stage almost at will or, on the other hand, compulsively?

As infants and youths develop, they are subjected to a wide variety of tests, some of which are formally designated as such. And while there is at least some validity to many of the practical and also formal tests, I query what the "results" tell us about the person. I suggest that "intelligence" is a function of synchronizing the cusp of personality (P-T-R) with the narrow task at hand or more broadly the ambience of that person. Success or failure may not be so much the innate potential ability but more a question of synchronization not just of the putative task but also with the additional messages attached to the narrowly defined task. Many truly brilliant people are pathetically stupid outside their very narrow cone of competence.

The emergence of the root P-T-R structure of the cusp of personality dictates the range of skill sets a person may have. The reason why some persons can eventually overcome a deficiency lies in whether a branch of loops is amenable to additional icons. For an icon to fit into a cusp of personality there must be corresponding interfaces on the respective loops. Thus, "how educable a person is" is a direct function of the number of open interfacing sites on the loops in that person's cusp of personality. Therefore, timelines could be deduced from mathematical models of the growth of the Gordian Knots of the variety of cusps of personality.

The scaffolding of the mind is largely completed by young adulthood; what education does thereafter is to fill the scaffolding with content (which is not the same thing as meaning). Meaning for any person is the junction of that person's scaffolding and a particular set of content. Somewhat analogous is the jury instruction to the effect that a question or an answer without the other is not evidence for a jury to consider but a question coupled with the responding answer is evidence for consideration.

THE ARGUMENT

THE ARGUMENT BEGAN in September, 1963, during my very first lesson in geometry as instructed by a math teacher named Stephen Chandler at The Mercersburg Academy. He introduced Euclid by the postulate: "There exists a point." Without hesitating, I asked him: "Why?" That query was a first taste of the conundrum that posed as my formal education.

Euclid, as least as taught by Stephen Chandler, sets the standard for reducing philosophy to a single proposition. By the way, my only formal instruction in classical philosophy, in particular Socratic logic, was provided by Alden Mosshammer, also at The Mercersburg Academy. His course was comprehensive enough that it included Buddhism upon which I wrote a term paper in early 1966. While I was at Cornell University, I participated in an applied philosophy course regarding the conservation of natural resources.

To answer my own question of "why?," I argue that all multi-propositional philosophies can be reduced by using the P-T-R nutcracker on each of philosophy's propositions to reach the point of pure human reason. By disentangling the loops through reiterative regression, one can discover the original organizing impulse; thus, solving the Gordian Knot riddle.

The rules applicable to such an analysis are:

1. Every thought is a loop composed of varying combinations of P, T & R.

2. Statements are always loops, not freestanding absolutes that many people take them to be.

3. Every component of a loop is a loop itself.

The primary cusp distribution may be 1/3, 1/3 & 1/3 but I believe that the distribution is skewed towards T and away from R. The predominate channel of communication between persons is the T - P channel or wavelength. The investigation of nature is R, but the communications between scientists are not necessarily so.

The mind processes perceptions simultaneously in three modes; reality is composed of those same elements and reality exists, as well, in three modes. The accuracy of perception is determined by how closely aligned the subjective P-T-R is with behavior of the external phenomena. All statements, written or oral, are transmitted simultaneously via three channels; all statements are received simultaneously in three channels. However, the corresponding channels are not necessarily in tune or are otherwise misaligned with each other because, once a message is received, the Mobius loops process the message with the Mobius loops' own coding.

UNIFICATION THEORY

A primer explicating the vectors that shape our lives should coherently weave together the roots of psychology, philosophy, politics, law, economics and policy. A philosophy needs to be comprehensive; otherwise, a purported philosophy is simply a collection, perhaps an encyclopedia, of many beliefs. A unified philosophy is a philosophy for all seasons of life. Elemental analysis is a Euclidean geometry of the mind premised on postulates and developed through logic toward a comprehensive and unified model of the mind. Unification theory is not confined to reductionism such as I am arguing. An alternative approach to unification is the "glass bead game" which involves the manipulations of symbols such that parallels or equivalencies are deduced. See Herman Hesse's Das Glasperlenspiel (1943).

The concept of a unified mind is a conundrum that needs to be parsed to be understood. Broadly speaking, unification theory is based on the two premises that, one, the mind accesses, or is at least capable of accessing, its full range of information and, two, that human minds follow the same developmental rules regardless of race or culture.

An error that I made for much of my life was believing that the mind could compile information not only logically but also rationally. That proposition has failed me time and time again. The failure lies in the mind. For notwithstanding that it is unified, the mind communicates within itself via some form of statement. On the premise that these communications are in the form of statements, then it is inevitable that the mind will misunderstand, misinterpret or otherwise fail at the task of rationally compiling information. The same sort of errors that occur in interpersonal communications occur in intrapersonal communications. Such failures in the internal communications is one of the sources for errors in misinterpreting what can otherwise be in a physical sense clearly observed.

Elemental analysis is a form of reductionism in contrast to an all embracing encyclopedic (mapping) vision of reality. Reductionism is found in many forms, some quite useful such as chemistry but other quite misleading and even malevolent such as Der Fuhrer principle espoused in the Third Reich. Can a reductionist concept be merged into an all embracing vision of reality? The Buddhist concept of OM is one such candidate. Abraham Maslow argued, at least implicitly, that well-integrated persons live positive (i.e., "good") lives. See the discussion of peak experiences and self-actualization in, inter alia, Toward a Psychology of Being (1962, 1968). For a countervailing argument that well-integrated persons are not necessarily good and that evil is not necessarily expunged from the psyche by self-actualization, see Winston L. King's "Zen and the Way of the Sword: Arming the Samurai Psyche" (1993). Japan's attack on Pearl Harbor (December 7, 1941) was a classic blunder induced by doctrine rather than national interest. Japan's national interest could have been well served by a less doctrinaire approach to diplomacy and negotiation. Policy and philosophy are obverse sides of the same coin of belief. Policy is a continuation of argument by other means (ala Carl von Clausewitz' dictum that war is the continuation of politics by different means; see Vom Kriege [1832]). Difficulties in making the peace arise when a counter party retains an attachment to an originating conflict event or misunderstanding.

DIRECT OBSERVATION

Naturalists, a term much broader than field biologists, are direct observers of natural phenomena. Naturalists should not be confused with naturists who have their own practice of direct observation. I tend to use the term naturalist in preference to scientist because scientists seem to focus on narrow tranches of inquiry. Naturalists try to grasp nature in its grandest form but in doing so are susceptible to committing errors in interpretation. Mathematicians are logicians and complement the naturalists in creating meaningful models.

Although science is a synonym for knowledge, I also tend to use the term naturalist rather than scientist because I prefer to restrict the term scientist for a practitioner of the scientific method that is rigorously confined to controlled experiments. Science, as defined by the scientific method of controlled experiments, is a very narrow tranche of the practice of "science" as that term is colloquially used. Once a scientist is doing something outside of controlled experiments, elements of policy intrude and may even dominate that practice.

The enhancement or subjective interpretation of photographs and other direct observation converts evidence into statements. You may want to review the history of the discussions of the photographic evidence regarding the deflection of light by the Sun as purportedly confirming Einsteinian relativity by Arthur Eddington during the May 29, 1919, solar eclipse. The starting point would be F. W. Dyson, A. S. Eddington and C. Davidson, A determination of the deflection of light by the Sun's gravitational field, from observations made at the total eclipse of 29 May 1919,"

Philosophical Transactions of the Royal Society 220A: 291-333 (1920). Images, whether items exhibited in a museum, a photograph, a set of photographs, a cinema, become symbols when an observer perceives an internal dynamic within himself vis-a-vis those images. That internal dynamic is ruled by the laws of P-T-R.

Observing nature directly means to look at natural phenomena as original propositions, almost as if through an infant's eyes, and not as reflections or simple-minded reaffirmations of statements made by some other observer, writer or commentator. Query: Is it possible to directly observe the mind in the manner of the great natural scientists, such as Galileo and Darwin, who have directly observed nature? The naturalists looked outward, but the task at hand is to look inward.

Direct observation is the act of observing phenomena and using the phenomena to acquire an understanding of the thing observed in contrast to having a set of beliefs by which to categorize the assorted wool gathered in the course of one's life. In the direct observation of nature, the great natural scientists made note of the wrinkles, creases and joints in the face of nature, looking for, if you will, inconsistencies in the word of God. Having noted the telling details, the great natural scientists developed analytical models that went far beyond simple equivalency. These scientists worked their models rather than deviate from the models' internal logics.

There is a scene in the movie The Big Short (screenplay by Charles Randolph and Adam McKay based upon the book by Michael Lewis; 05/11/2015 buff revision pp. 23, 23A & 24) inside a yeshiva where the mother of a 10 year old boy is discussing her son with the rabbi:

Rabbi: …Mark…is the best student of the Torah and the Talmud…

Mother: Then what's the problem Rabbi?

Rabbi: It's the reason.. He says he studies so hard because…he is looking for inconsistencies in the word of God.

Mother: So has he found any?

Inherent ambiguities in perception bedevil everyone in all activities of life. My sister, your Aunt Gloria, argued in the preface to the published edition of her doctoral thesis on Renaissance art, specifically that of Luca Signorelli, that "The large questions of meaning thus avoided are precisely the ones which we should risk."

A classic and tragic example of simple equivalency was Bruno Bettelheim's assertion that mothers who withheld emotional nourishment from their children (so called "refrigerator mothers") caused their children to be autistic. Bruno Bettelheim (1903-1990) was incarcerated in the Dachau and Buchenwald concentration camps from 1938 to 1939. While there, he directly observed the dire states of mind of the prisoners which were quite reasonably attributable to concentration camp conditions. He at some much later point in time came to the conclusion that those states of mind were equivalent to what he observed directly in children whom he believed were autistic. He thereupon propounded the bogus theory that autism was caused by mothers withholding emotional nourishment to their children. This simple minded nonsense was widely accepted by practicing physicians and psychologists in the 1950s and 1960s and great harm was done to rather than help provided to autistic children and their families.

To directly observe or experience nature is a task that is not necessarily intuitively obvious. In the sport of fly fishing for trout, a distinction is made between "wild" fish and "hatchery" fish. A spectacular rainbow trout sport fishery exists in the San Juan River tailwater of Navajo Dam in northwestern New Mexico. That fishery was created and maintained by the stocking of rainbow trout following the construction of the dam; i.e., it is not a "natural" or "wild" fishery. To an extent, it has been a "put-and-take" fishery with a delay between the "putting" of small trout and the harvesting, after time and growth, of large trout. [Current regulations are "catch-and-release" rather than bagging a harvested trout.] In a different vein, the name of the New Mexico city Truth or Consequences has nothing to do with the administration of criminal justice in the tradition of dime novels and the romance of the Old West. The city changed its name from Hot Springs in 1950 in order to win a television quiz show challenge to adopt the quiz show's name (Truth or Consequences) as the city's name.

Thus, there are nuances in how we experience nature or the manufactured equivalent. "What is real and what is imagination?" is a question addressed by Damien Hirst in his cinema "Treasures from the Wreck of the Unbelievable" (2017).

A tangent of the same question is to what extent can a direct experience be preserved? In the modern era of taxidermy, there is nothing in a wall-mounted trout that is from the fish itself other than its image transferred into a fiberglass replica.

Can you distinguish an illusion from the event? An illusion is a verbally encoded screen, a filter; an event itself is unreduced to verbal form. Direct observation generates creases in understanding that can be profitably explored. Essentially, a crease is an unanticipated event. Examples include the rats' response when then graduate student B. F. Skinner failed to maintain the feeding schedule and another was Niko Tinbergen putting an equal number of male and female sticklebacks in an aquarium and, subsequently, observing more female than male sticklebacks in the exact same population of individuals.

Fear is specifically a sense of potentially losing control. Persons may have few or many fears but it would be an error is to describe a person as having a fearful disposition. In other words, fear is not an innate characteristic but merely a product of reacting to an image that signifies in some way helplessness. The remedy for a fear is to develop competence specific to the dilemma behind the mask of that fear.

Is it better to have forgotten than remember? Is remembering an illusion as the event itself a form of forgetting? Akira Kurosawa viewed, at the insistence of his older brother Heigo, the devastation of Tokyo caused by the 1923 earthquake and resulting fires. "The worst was when we stood on the bank of the red-dyed Sumida River and gazed at the throng of corpses pressed against its shore. I felt my knees give way as I started to faint, but my brother grabbed me by the collar and propped me up again. He repeated, 'Look carefully, Akira.'" … "Kurosawa returned to his home that night, certain he would be unable to sleep. He awaited a procession of nightmares but instead slept soundly, which he thought so strange that he asked his brother about it. … Heigo's reply: 'If you shut your eyes to a frightening sight, you end up being frightened. If you look at everything straight on, there is nothing to be afraid of.'" Paul Anderer, *Kurosawa's Rashomon: a vanished city, a lost brother, and the voice inside his iconic films* (2016) pp. 30 & 31.

THE TRI-PARTITE MIND

Life as defined by our minds is multi-dimensional. I do not know the number of dimensions, which must be at least three, but I do not want to propound a silly ad infinitum dimensional model. The model itself may generate nodes of information ad infinitum but I think that the dimensions, the scaffolding, must be finite.

We in our daily lives carry on often in one-dimension (as a soldier obeying an order), two dimensions (thoughtful shopping as opposed to compulsive purchasing), and three dimensions (comprehensive investigation of retirement relocation). Few individuals, other than scholarly mathematicians and physicists, ever get beyond three dimensional thinking.

There are abundant anecdotal examples of the expressions of the tri-partite mind; these examples suggest or imply that the structure of any problem must conform to the three elements. John Maynard Keynes described "the political problem of mankind" as being "how to combine three things: economic efficiency, social justice and individual liberty." At first cut, one might ascribe the R element to economic efficiency, T to social justice and P to individual liberty. As one might pursue second, third, et al. levels of analysis, presumably the meshing and divisions within political economy would be revealed as a description of political life. Tri-partite patterns are evident in the Chayes, Ehrlich & Lowenfeld materials regarding the Cuban Missile Crisis (International Legal Process, 1968).

There may be a correspondence between the model of the tri-partite mind and Zen's three seed syllables (OM, AH & HUM). See S. van Schaik's Tibetan Zen: discovering a lost tradition p. 187 (2015). Similarly, there may be a correspondence between the tri-partite mind and Buddhist Tantra practice. "We practice Chenrezig to develop loving-kindness and compassion; Manjushri for wisdom, sharpness of intellect, and clarity of mind; and Vajrapani to develop power, the capacity to be potent, effective, and confident." Rob Preece, The Psychology of Buddhist Tantra p. 57 (2000, 2006). The corresponding seed syllables, being the innate vibrations underlying all phenomena and often express through mantras, are HRIH, DHIH and TAM. Id., p. 98 & 99.

Examples, such as the three Fates (Clotho, Lachesis and Atropos) occur in mythology. See the end note, infra, re the Seventh Preface, supra.

My favorite example of the cultural expression of the tri-partite mind is the trio of the Cowardly Lion, the Tin Man and the Scarecrow in The Wizard of Oz (cinema) (1939) which was based on the book The Wonderful Wizard of Oz (1900) (and perhaps other books in the series) by L. Frank Baum. The inverse correspondence (between the element and the characteristic that the character lacks) would be P and the Lion (courage), T and the Tin Man (heart), and R with the Scarecrow (a brain).

THE PROBABILITY OF TRUTHFUL STATEMENTS

A narrator or an interlocutor is unreliable in that he speaks symbolically rather than purely literally. The limits of conversation were alluded to in

Ernest Hemingway's For Whom the Bell Tolls (1940) in which the protag-
onist Robert Jordon characterized dealing with the guerrilla leader Pablo
as a merry-go-round.

Even if all participants in a conversation are speaking the same language, say American English, what is being said needs to individually
translated through elemental analysis for any individual to comprehend
the range of content in the conversation. Ordinary statements are inherently ambiguous and misleading. There are no free standing true statements. No one statement can completely incorporate its meanings and no
set of statements can completely incorporate their collective meanings.

In order to understand the message, you must decode the image or
icon. Many people hear so clearly because they hear so little. If psychoanalysis is in fact a "talking cure", a term coined by Josef Breuer's patient Anna
O. (Bertha Pappenheim), then the very nature of the form of statements is
central to that process.

If all statements are composed, at the initial "facial" level of analysis,
of three alternative dominant elements, and each statement is read through
a lens of three alternative elements, the probability of truth (using the analogy that it is the "question AND its answer" that constitutes evidence in
judicial trials) being stated in the normal course of events is about 11% (1/3
x 1/3 = 1/9 [.33 x .33 = .11]).

This conjecture is inapplicable where the statements are highly
defined, such as in mathematical proofs. I do not see the conjecture as anything other than a rule of thumb implied by the basic model. What I see
useful in it is the realization that the vast majority of statements are not
truthful and, if not lies, then misleading partial statements resulting in, if
not tragedy, then a Comedy of Errors. I like to think that Diogenes, who
jokingly searched with a lantern for an honest man, would agree.

Consider the probability proposition in construing or mis-constru-
ing the United States Constitution and its Amendments. My observation
goes to the nub of the argument between the strict (original intent)

constructionists and those who believe in interpreting the Constitution as an organic document that grows alongside American society. For a stark example of this debate regarding the right to bear arms, see Carl T. Bogus' The Hidden History of the Second Amendment, U.C. Davis Law Review, vol. 31, no. 2 (1998) p. 309 et seq. which is an excellent example of exegesis clarifying a conundrum of a statement. What is so compelling about Bogus' thesis is that it explains the peculiar syntax of the Second Amendment which is otherwise subject to tortured interpretations of its facial meaning.

An ultimate limit on the truth of statements is that tertiary concepts are collapsed into binary statements. Truthful statements are at least tertiary but we tend to interpret statements as binary. The most famous discussion of this phenomenon is that by Plato reporting in his Republic Socrates' Allegory of the Cave with its shadows on the wall.

Sentences are fragments of thought. Actions other than physiological or reflexive actions are also fragments of thought. While sentences and actions may appear to be conclusions and therefore complete, they are nonetheless fragmentary. It is impossible for a statement standing by itself to be complete or to be universally true. As additional statements are appended to a statement, the statement approaches completeness but can not achieve completeness. Every individual speaks in code, his own language, because each person developed his own language skills by the unique sequence and pattern of his development. Seeing, hearing and other sensory perceptions are subject to encoding errors creating differences between the perceptions and the objective stimuli. The answer to why a deviation from a standard, expectation or ideal occurs is found in how the deviation arose through its antecedent vectors. We speak in icons, created by the speaker and interpreted by the listener. In order to understand irrationality, or perhaps even some forms of insanity, one needs to understand icons and symbols because it is the correspondence between some act, phrase or item and some construct of our own mind that can run us off the road into a ditch where we spin our wheels.

ALTERNATE REALITIES

How many lives can one person live in? How many realities? How many worlds? How many lives do you live? How do you know what you know and why do you believe what you know? There is no pre-ordaining that one's cusp of personality will be congruent with the dynamics of the physical and social realities of life. To the extent of one being totally congruent, then one is an automaton, a cyborg. To the extent that one diverges from congruity, one is to some degree insane. Your cusp of personality with its predominant trait determines how you initially read or interpret a statement or action, which affects spontaneity as well as subsequent analysis and processing.

Alternate realities are defined by their predominant mode (P, T or R) of organization. They exist, not as mysticism or fantasy, but as different rules. For as many alternate realities you care to find, there will exist a set of rules that defines each realm. All of the realms are elementally analyzable. As best as I can tell, elemental analysis (P-T-R) is a straight forward explanation of "multiple personalities." Alternate realities degrees of difference or separation are measured by the number of P-T-R loops in the transformation from one reality to another. Metaphorically, these degrees can be visualized as Monet's Water Lilies or, if you prefer, an actual lily pond.

The alternative reality concept is simply a function of the tri-partite structure of sentience at the level of consciousness. Schrodinger's Cat comes to mind as an example of, in Schrodinger's choice of word, Verschrankung (entanglement). Fred Alan Wolf has been a proponent of the bridge between physics, specifically quantum mechanics, and consciousness. In a 2010 letter to my brother Wendell, I noted that:

"On a psychological-philosophical perspective, I am not yet convinced of Wolf's most fundamental argument re consciousness. I do not reject it out-of-hand and I almost concede that it must play some role but I think that there must be more to it than that.

However, the [Wolf's] argument served as a tangent takeoff for a riff of thought about how we compose reality through our feelings of what we think we perceive. In that sense, we do live simultaneous multiple lives and for one factor or another select a life we understand. I see our living simultaneous multiple lives as a phenomenon that is not influenced or otherwise controlled by quantum mechanics."

Novels present alternate realities, not just in the overall presentation but also internally. D. H. Lawrence's Women in Love (1920) presents a clash in alternate realities in the juxtaposition of the four principal personas. In reading text or any other verbal message, there are, in addition to just reading it, three analytical ways to proceed: read the images (T) or the relationships (P) or the logic (R). If one had the time and the patience to read a novel three times, one could first read it focusing on the imagery, in the second reading you could key on the relationships and, thirdly, one might then exegete the logic, particularly the internal logic.

The Humpty Dumpty Challenge: Having deconstructed your reality into its elements, is it possible to construct a new, different, reality for yourself? I.e., can the elements be put back together in a different manner so as to create a coherent whole persona other than the one you already have? We all live, or attempt to live, in a reality that corresponds with the strongest element in our individual cusp of personality. We can travel to and through other realities premised on our minor elements, but we are uncomfortable and eventually revert to our preferred reality. Your preferred reality is your safe harbor, your bulwark against your failure in your other realities. That these alternative realities exist is the ultimate reason why unification theory fails for individuals on a practical, day-to-day continuum. In navigating through the alternate realities, bear in mind the keys to maintaining your sanity are to understand your own cusp of personality and to use the tools of elemental analysis to decipher your present predicament.

I participated in a training exercise during a continuing legal education program regarding negotiation skills. In this moot court simulation, the ostensible task was to conduct a settlement negotiation regarding a commercial lawsuit over the delivery of non-conforming goods. In the time frame of the program, about an hour, the participants needed to review the case materials, prepare a negotiation strategy and then to conduct the negotiation. I, in fact, developed a position and a set of tactics designed to settle the lawsuit. When the results of all of the other negotiations were compared, I was stunned to learn that I missed the opportunity to create huge value for my client because I focused narrowly on the ostensible subject of negotiation, the lawsuit, as the task at hand and did not see that the lawsuit presented an opportunity for a much greater business purpose. Some of the other program participants saw the business opportunity and pursued a grander negotiation strategy than I did.

This experience is a demonstration of the phenomenon of simultaneous multiple realities (at least at the point of opportunity or point of sale): same facts, different perceptions, different outcomes. The program was Gain the Edge: negotiation strategies for lawyers by Martin E. Latz (December 12, 2017, at Melville, New York) under the sponsorship of the New York State Bar Association.

The game of chess provides a demonstration that perception of physical reality differs among individuals, sometimes attributed to "talent". Persons with functioning vision, a player's understanding of the rules, and an opportunity to learn through experience will vary considerably in the rate of growth of their skill and eventually the level of expertise they achieve. A similar phenomenon occurs in students studying mathematics. In the case of chess, what becomes a limiting factor is the ability to read or see the board, i.e., observe and comprehend what is in plain sight. The chess pieces are easily physically seen by a player but not all are comprehended. In effect, players with different abilities to read the board are playing different games, i.e., playing in different realities. The different abilities are innate and once an individual approaches his limit he can go no further except in adopting memorized work-arounds. Work-arounds are devices or shortcuts that allow an individual to benefit from more sophisticated knowledge by assuming that the knowledge is true and then utilizing that knowledge's rubrics.

If you do not understand something that might be considered common knowledge by others, it is not necessarily because of ignorance or lack of intelligence on your part but could simply be that your perception is providing you with alternative signals. The question for you then becomes one of reading your own signals. The tension between a "unified mind" and alternate realities is caused by the predominant element in a cusp of personality trying to recast the other elements into itself. Whenever the mind perceives anything, it simultaneously encodes it in the three modes although one or two of the modes may be in the subconscious or unconscious. Thus, a fervent belief based on one mode can eventually be undone by the emergence of the alternative modes. The tragic comedy of life is that, notwithstanding the thoughts of the mind, life events occur outside the mind which forces the great reduction of, at least potentially, complex thoughts to simple "truths" and acts. A different question is presented by what are appropriate perceptions of one's habitat in its physical, chemical and biological interfaces.

I argue that the carousel-Ferris wheel model provides an explanation for memory mobility as well as the malleability of memories. Memory is not confined to one locus in the brain. The location of a memory appears either to be mobile or concurrently existing in multiple loci, which might partially account for concurrent alternative memories. Whether the brain shifts a memory among alternative loci or selectively activates a locus among multiple loci may be testable by comparing the elemental accents of alternative concurrent memories, i.e., whether the theme emphasis is power or identity or reason.

Query: Can two or more communities with the same individuals exist in the same time and place? I.e., can multiple communities be truly simultaneous? There are well known stages of infant play (unoccupied play, solitary play, onlooker play, parallel play, associative play, cooperative play) that correspond with the growth and development of the P-T-R structure of the infant's mind. The stage of parallel play is particularly intriguing as the model for adults "talking past each other", i.e., having a conversation without engagement. Query whether many adults have ever progressed beyond associative play to cooperative play. Do adults yo-yo between the infant development stages? Perhaps acting momentarily in one stage but reverting to another stage almost at will or, on the other hand, compulsively? Rational people do not do well in social settings because the logic of social settings is based on a model dominated by P and T elements. In sorting out any sense of failure on your own part, look at the core cusp of personality within yourself. Since there are many "correct" ways of perception, that one's preferred mode of perception differs from that of others in his community does not means the the person is necessarily insane or incompetent. Galen Strawson in his Things That Bother Me: death, freedom, the self, etc. (2018) at p. 46 agrees in principle: "I don't think it's true that there is only one way in which human beings experience their being in time, and only one good way for them to do this." The cultural-social amalgam may very well treat harshly those persons with otherwise naturally occurring beliefs. That harsh treatment begs the question of who is insane: the inquisitor or the heretic?

SEXUALITY

Sex is a wild card in human relations, largely because there can be extraordinary meta-sexual implications and ramifications resulting from sexual acts. Sexual thoughts and sexual behavior are both easily modeled through elemental analysis, perhaps because sex is primeval. The characterization of Freudian theory as "sexual" as opposed to some form of enlightenment may be an appropriate focus. One could choose sex, say as opposed to dreams, as the first door towards analysis. There are other candidates for "first doors." However, many of the other candidates are more difficult to utilize directly because they are in part later products of the mental scaffolding rather than appearing as forces in the scaffolding itself.

In terms of ontogeny, the development of the P-T-R structure precedes the emergence of any form of sexuality in an individual and thereby provides the framework for the Freudian mind (and not vice versa). Sex is an exploration of one's mind as much as it is of one's body. The stages of ontogeny in infancy and adolescence are well known but ontogeny does not stop at the age of emancipation; ontogeny continues but not in so predictable ways. Our adult growth depends on how stymied we are by fixations at any stage. Some go on; others stay.

One source of the wild card aspect of sexuality in humans is that hormonal cycles of males and females are different lengths, perhaps 3 or 4 days in males and about 28 days in females. Thus, the cycles are inherently asynchronous. As these hormonal cycles emerge in adolescent development, the thought processes adapt the imbalance as a model for mediation of all other matters between the sexes which leads to the phenomenon, as a general rule with many exceptions, that women choose their mates rather than vice-versa. Although overt sexual forces are developmentally and hormonally driven, the variations in their expressions are P-T-R statements and are, in some sense, forms of alternate realities.

RELIGION

There are many parallels, perhaps links, between and among religions and philosophies but not all supposed links are worthy of pursuit. D.T.Suzuki in his Introduction to Zen Buddhism (1934) suggested that the Christian philosopher Tertullian's argument in De Carne Christi for the belief in Christ's transformation following his crucifixion (being the primary basis of Christian faith), to wit: "prorsus credible est, quia ineptum est" (it is by all means to be believed, because it is absurd) and "certum est, quit impossibile" (it is certain, because impossible) as an "unqualified confirmation of Zen." Suzuki's suggestion in the form of the query "is this not an unqualified confirmation of Zen?" is a disservice to both Christianity and Zen Buddhism. To defend the absurdities in one's set of beliefs is simply to defend one's own sense of identity.

Gods exist only in our minds, regardless of whether one was indoctrinated with a monotheistic or polytheistic religion. Monotheism attempts to unify the mind with a doctrinaire structure, perhaps modeled on a parents-child-family image. The defect in monotheism is that the mind's structure is created before the individual experiences family life or religious training and indoctrination. Polytheistic religions more broadly correspond with the structure of the mind with the different "gods" corresponding with different sets of P-T-R allowing different personalities to emerge and be accommodated within such religions. Polytheistic religions are, thus, more forgiving of transgressions as transgressions are inherently partial rather than absolute. Similarly, unified political and social systems are less tolerant of diversity than open political and social systems that encompass multiple values.

Zen meditation and psychoanalysis, notwithstanding similarities as methods of introspection, are not identical (I.e., there is no one-to-one correspondence between them). Zen devolves to the realization of universal abstracts while analysis reaches for originating individual events.

Are analogous religious beliefs and practices, such as ephemeral sand painting, the product of being derived by tradition from a single origin? Or, do the analogous beliefs and practices arise from the endogenous mind? Tibetan and Southwestern Native American sand paintings are certainly analogous. The Tibetan and Native American peoples share a common ancestry before the exodus across the Siberia-Alaska bridge approximately 10,000 years ago. Query whether the thoughts underpinning sand painting are tradition or, alternatively, independently arising from the mind.

A recurring debate occurs between fundamentalists who rely on a supposed literal reading of religious texts and others who see religious texts as a source of inspiration and guidance. The complexity of the intertwining of religious belief and what sort of life one chooses to lead is peculiarly demonstrated by Clarence Darrow's cross-examination of William Jennings Bryan in the Scopes Trial in Dayton, Tennessee in July of 1925. In essence, the cross-examination exposed the lack of logic in accepting a literal interpretation of the Christian Bible, in particular the Book of Genesis. What may not be obvious is that, notwithstanding the characterization of Bryan as a Bible thumping buffoon, Bryan was otherwise a humanist who truly cared for the welfare of ordinary people. While other commentators may use Bryan's "Cross of Gold" speech (at the Democratic National Convention in Chicago on July 9, 1896, as well as on many other occasions) as the best evidence for his humanism, I would select his action of resigning on June 9, 1915, as President Woodrow Wilson's Secretary of State in protest of what Bryan believed to be the prelude of the United States entering the war in Europe.

As a obiter dictum, I should mention that a similar controversy exists regarding the interpretation of the United States Constitution. In an overly simplified way, the two major competing schools of thought are composed of those scholars and jurists who believe that the Constitution should be interpreted and applied with commonsense in recognizing the organic growth of American society and those scholars and jurists who purport to be strict constructionists who insist that, in the absence of amendment, the Constitution must be interpreted and applied according to the intent of the persons who drafted and institutionalized the Constitution. The strict constructionists' argument fails for many reasons not the least of which is they do not practice what they preach. A clear demonstration of their hypocrisy is the strict constructionists in applying the Second Amendment regarding the bearing of arms conveniently ignore that the original purpose of the Second Amendment was to allay the fear in the slave holding states that the federal government would attempt to disarm the state militias, which at that time were perceived by the slave holders as their bulwark against slave revolts. See Carl T. Bogus' The Hidden History of the Second Amendment, U.C. Davis Law Review, vol. 31, no. 2 (1998) p. 309 et seq. Carl Bogus concluded (p. 408) that "the Second Amendment lives two lives: one in the law and the other in politics, public policy, and popular culture. The hidden history has ramifications in the second realm as well. The Second Amendment takes on an entirely different complexion when instead of being symbolized by a musket in the hands of the minuteman, it is associated with a musket in the hands of the slave holder."

An analogous question concerning the reading of foundational documents arose in the Ninth Century during which Muslims (perhaps influenced by Greek philosophy) debated whether the Koran was given as the word of God or created as representative of the word of God. If sanctified as given, then the reading of the Koran is fundamental and absolute; if created, then reading the Koran becomes dynamic and subject to interpretation.

Students, at least in America, are commonly introduced to philosophy by reading and discussing Plato's works regarding Socrates (Euthyphro, Apology, Crito and Phaedo) as well as Plato's magnum opus Republic and his archetype of debate Symposium. Consider as an alternative approach to the same character of philosophical inquiry the Dunhuang cave manuscripts of Tibetan Zen. See Sam van Schaik's Tibetan Zen: discovering a lost tradition (2015). One of the phenomena of religions is that schisms develop within them over time. While van Schaik's book is exclusively focused on Zen Buddhism, many of his observations are useful in understanding the schisms that have occurred in Christianity and Islam as well as other religions.

My argument for an "internal logic of the mind" is incongruent with the "enlightened nothingness" of Zen. I see this incongruence not as a contradiction but as a difference in cones of focus. I believe that a Buddhist guru would say that the internal logic of the mind falls short of enlightenment thus arising to a cusp whereby one can embrace enlightenment only by abandoning elemental analysis and crossing over to the universe of OM.

PHILOSOPHY & POLICY

Treatises on policy have been written in literate bureaucratic societies. Kautilya' Arthashastra (The Science of Politics) appeared two millennia ago in India; Niccolò Machiavelli's Il Principe (The Prince) was published in 1532 in Italy. A classical question in policy studies is whether a person or entity is stronger by accumulating power by dominating or excluding others or by sharing power. The answer in the short run is to accumulate power at the expense of others but the answer in the long run is to share power. An illustrative example is Britain's present strength in the international community and its prior empire. Britain's colonial policy was to accumulate wealth and power at the expense of its colonies. The Americans revolted and eventually emerged as a powerful ally with a "special relationship" with Britain. Compare whether Britain's present international status is enhanced by any comparable relationship with India which emerged from Britain's colonial rule in 1947 against the wishes of Winston Churchill. A useful exercise in policy studies would be to compare the views of noted leaders regarding national self-interest and colonial rule. Start with Tojo, Churchill and FDR and make your own conclusions as who had a better grasp of policy and national self-interest.

The prevalence of lying is that people are uncomfortable with their abilities to address reality and truth. Lying is a convenient "out" delaying or avoiding the consequences of the work to be rational and humanistic. Lying is an implicit acknowledgment by the prevaricator to himself that he is weak, that he lacks the ability to work through the problem at hand. "Statesmen will invent cheap lies, putting blame upon the nation that is attacked, and everyman will be glad of those conscience-soothing falsities, and will diligently study them, and refuse to examine any refutations of them; and thus he will by and by convince himself that the war is just, and will thank God for the better sleep he enjoys after this process of grotesque self-deception." Mark Twain, The Chronicle of Young Satan (1897-1900).

The "best and brightest," the Eastern Establishment, and other "highly qualified" labels are misleading because all of the members of the club are, in fact, ordinary people who respond to cues rather than objective analysis. These hard-headed realists often turn out to be stupid romantics responding to some image and supposed calling that leads to strategic blunders in places like Viet Nam and Iran as well as the interface of micro and macro economics leading to the farce of bailing out banks in the 2008 crisis of the banks' own making. The bulk of the so-called hard-headed realists' decisions are predominately based on emotions (T and P) with R being relegated to a very narrow scope of vision.

Military conflicts often have counterintuitive consequences. The Indian-Chinese Border War (1959-1962) resulted in a military victory by the Chinese that was followed by the Chinese declaring a unilateral cease-fire and withdrawing its military forces to territory occupied by the Chinese prior to the beginning of the hostilities. See Ramachandra Guha, India After Gandhi (2007, chapter 15 The Experience of Defeat pp. 306-341). The resolution of this conundrum undoubtedly lies in the internal politics of China. Internal or domestic politics can give rise to military excursions that are not justified by self-defense. India seized by military force (Operation Vijay) the Portuguese colony of Goa in 1961 to bolster the electoral prospects of Krishna Menon, the Indian Minister of Defense who played a weak hand on behalf of India in its Himalayan dispute with China. See Guha, supra, pp. 331-333. Argentina, in an attempt to uphold the domestic standing of its generals, attempted to seize in 1982 what it called the Malvinas Islands but which were held as the Falkland Islands by Britain. The Argentinian excursion was a failure. Once you base war on a domestic agenda, then you are conducting war for the prince and not the people. Arriving there, you enter the world of psychology, the prince initially and the people subsidiarily. You are now home in the realm of elemental analysis.

Your cusp of personality is your functional, perhaps unstated, philosophy of life. What you may declare as your philosophy of life may bear little resemblance to your operational philosophy. A philosopher's philosophy is generated by his personal psychology. All reasons exist only in the form of statements, which are inherently incomplete. Authority is the end of reason, the stop sign in argument. Chains of thought are concluded by the coup de grace of authority (power; "P") which exists as self contained and complete, which gives rise to Der Fuhrer principle, Operation Barbarosso, German concentration camps and the Gulf of Tonkin Resolution. Thus, the German Volk's complicity in the Nazis' crimes against humanity and American fathers sending their sons to Viet Nam. In a sense, authoritarianism arises out of the first stimulus in utero that organizes the emerging cusp of personality in that the other elements organize themselves in response to the assertion of the event which in later life is transfigured into the assertion of authority that causes otherwise rational people to subvert their own identity by the rationalization away of reason.

Politics and economics are intimately intertwined. Excellent economic analysis (R) should serve as a check on political passions (P and T). Examples include Adam Smith's The Wealth of Nations (1776) as an argument against mercantilism; John Maynard Keynes' The Economic Consequences of the Peace (1919) as an argument against onerous reparations following World War One; benefit-cost analysis as check on public investment in infrastructure such as dams. In re the latter, see, e.g., Otto Eckstein, Water Resource Development: the economics of project evaluation (1958). One of the checks that sound economic analysis provides is on the all too easily visualized exaggerations by local politicians of the benefits of invested dollars circulating in their regional economies. The metric is known as the "multiplier." By asserting fanciful multipliers, dam proponents could argue the justification for funding the building of their dam as revitalizing their regional economy by the circulation of the dollars within the local (regional) economy. It is easy to imagine that dollars paid as wages are spent and circulated several times within the community but accurate assessments indicate that the multiplier effect is quite modest (about 1.3).

The other side of the economics analysis coin is providing the theoretical rationale, much like a Brandeis Brief in law, for progressive income taxation based in part by the marginal utility of a dollar. The Brandeis Brief style of argument arose as a response to United States Supreme Court justices using narrow legal reasoning based on stare decisis to strike down progressive legislation (see, e.g., Lochner v. New York, 198 U.S. 45 [1905]) and thereby refusing to look at the actual consequences of over reliance on stare decisis. Louis Brandeis argued in Muller v. Oregon (208 U.S. 412 [1908]) for the constitutionality of progressive legislation and extensively relied on scientific and sociological information. The Supreme Court justices then looked, saw and decided based on reality and not doctrine.

All policy is psychology (P-T-R) because policy is a product of thought. Even the most extreme expression, as perhaps memorialized in or reduced to a "sophisticated financial instrument", is psychological in its elements. As rarefied as it may seem, after working from whatever initial thought you may have had through a series of loops (P-T-R), you arrive at the result (the instrument) which, of course, is an expression of P-T-R. Decisions, statements and actions are motivated by the symbols or icons that exist in our minds. Symbols that are physical objects constitute another meaning of the term. We do not conclude a process on reason alone, or, for that matter, identity or power, for it is the symbol or icon within our minds that seals the deal.

THE SOCIETAL MIND

The exploration of one's mind is, at least in stages, the exploration of not only one's self, but also all minds and one's family and society and, in more than a trivial way, the earth and the universe. Society replicates the mind; there is a one-to-one correspondence between social roles and the diverse portions of the tri-partite mind which is starkly evident in how the police and judiciary conduct themselves. Law is a lemma that mediates the passions (P & T) of society. The failure of law to fulfill its promises is because, by itself, the law can not impose its will; it must rely on the other elements which can deliberately distort what the law in the form of R is. There must be a correspondence between society and the human mind because, otherwise, society could not organize itself. The internal logic of the mind scales to the internal logic of society. This correspondence, this shared language and logic, is the conduit through which society communicates with individuals and vice-versa. Thus, societies provide maps of the mind, beginning with isolated individuals and small tribes progressing through larger and larger congeries reaching to organized societies and eventually large and complex empires of human endeavor. At least in theory, a researcher could map the correspondence between the model of the human mind and, say for example, the Roman Empire as it existed on March 15th in 44 B.C.

A cornucopia of candidates for societal correspondence exegesis exist. The Sunday editions of The New York Times and the Los Angeles Times could be mapped as mirrors of society. The mirrors metaphor is particularly apt if seen as sets of mirrors reflecting back and forth what exist between them. A physical model of this phenomenon was created by the extraordinarily large mirrors on opposing walls of the Luchow's Restaurant dining room (NYC, 1960s).

One of the peculiarities of societal roles that individuals largely self-select is that the predominant logic of the role roughly corresponds with the internal logic of the individual. By and large, of course with many exceptions, persons with a major P component to their cusps of personality would select roles as police officers, prosecutors and judges. Libertarian defense counsel would have a major R component and social defense counsel would have a major T component. In a phantasmagorical manner of speaking, society in the abstract can be visualized as an all encompassing (for that society) mind that directly corresponds in its organization, logic, vectors, etc. with those of an individual's mind. Obviously, with the scaling up, the societal mind is more comprehensive and complex than that of any one individual mind.

A peculiar aspect of Freud's quest to understand the human psyche is that he applied analytical logic to social logic. Analytical intelligence and social intelligence are two different forms of logic. Analytical intelligence is the ability (R) to process through levels of logic, whether quickly or over a very long period of time. Social intelligence is premised on one's acceptance of his "place" in his community's social order and is implemented through the logic of acceptance of "authority" (P) and bonding with other members in the community (T). Are problem solving skills scalable from micro through intermediate to macro? Additional factors emerge or disappear as scale changes; thus, the question becomes what factors drop out or come into play as scale changes? Note, that on a macro-societal scale, there is a social architecture that is far more complex than that of small groups which leads to a solution for individuals who find that they are incongruent with their purported peers.

One could argue that, analytical and social logics being different forms of logic, that they do not mix very well in practice, which leads to, among other things, the ostracism of Asperger endowed individuals from conventional social life. They live by different premises and rules. The social asymmetry results from them being in a small minority and the overwhelming majority, not understanding them, rejecting them, much like chimpanzees assaulting and killing a lone chimpanzee that wanders into their group from another tribe. How much is the attack premised on identity (T) and how much is premised on a lack of understanding (R)? One can easily believe that gang violence is preordained in any situation that a gang, being otherwise unoccupied in productive pursuits, perceive a signal, such as a red bandana being displayed by an individual, that the person is unworthy of respect in that a huge amount of prior accumulated belief is dumped onto that person through the symbol. The predominant force in society is the enforcement of the social order on a micro-societal basis, e.g., one-on-one interactions or the internal conduct of small groups. See, e.g., Jeffrey Gettleman & Suhasini Raj, "Caste Is Still Enforced in a Changing India, With Fists and Blades," The New York Times CLXVIII (no. 58,150) p.8 (Sunday, Nov. 18, 2018) reports an act of scalping to enforce the caste hierarchy in That, India, in September, 2018.

In an entirely different vein of thought, the two competing models of analytical intelligence and social intelligence explain the mediocrity of many college lecturers and instructors who deviate from the analytical logic of their disciplines and, for entertainment or some other reason, inject social logic. Social logic is rudimentary and repetitive and, while it enables individuals to advance themselves within society, it fails to provide the means to advance the knowledge and skills beyond the pale of the small group dynamics of a tribe.A Socratic Syndrome exists whereby philosophers, as well as those who are so inclined, as opposed to apologists, do not do well in bureaucracies.

Consensus logic is based on accepting what others say or do; analysis is based on the examination of the facts. The predominant mode of discussion is seeking a consensus through existing social conventions. Consensus thinking leads to the misinterpretation of human emotions, e.g., believing that a person is jealous just because he is critical. To ask questions that undermine not just the consensus but also social conventions is an irritant that lead many people to reject the truth of the inquiry and to expel the proponent. Thus, the trial of Socrates as well as the expulsion, banishment and killing of intellectuals during periods of revolution.Consensus is the default mode for making decisions; individuals vote into the consensus in order to avoid the work of analysis and to avoid the responsibility for undesirable consequences. You can measure and compare the workloads for analysis vs. consensus accepting freeloading (freeriding) by doing comparative P-T-R diagrams or outlines.

If you are disinclined towards introspection, a backdoor exists for you to understand your cusp of personality. Simply list the "terms of engagement" that you accept for social and societal interactions. Take your list and, for each item, determine whether the item is a greater / lesser, equal or query function. Cobble the items together as best you can for an overall function which, of course, corresponds with or is representative of your cusp of personality. You may also wish to compose a list for your tribe (which may be your family) as well as one for your broader society. Analyze each item as to its function and cobble together the lists for your tribe (or family) and your society. Compare the lists for yourself, your tribe (or family) and your society for a measure of your social dissonance.

A common standard within a social or tribal group is "traditional family values." Three observations are particularly worth noting. First, there is not a complete correspondence among the "traditional family values" of the diverse ethnic communities. Second, while traditional family values are enforced within a tribe, in complex societies composed of many tribes the rules of engagement for the complex society do not necessarily correspond with traditional family values. Third, individuals within any tribe may be innately predisposed to living life on terms at odds with his tribe, which typically leads to ostracism, banishment or, at a minimum, non-accommodation. Even if there is a uniformly accepted set of family values within a tribe, conflicts within a tribe are inevitable. A typical problem is jealousy.

Since individuals are resistant to thinking out problems, precedent within a family can set a standard of expectation for the generation approaching emancipation. Some fathers who did military service may find it hard to distinguish the circumstances of their service and the circumstances facing their sons. The acceptance of personal hardship, fear and risk of death is certainly appropriate under some circumstances. But the attitude of "I did my service and so should you" demonstrates the inability to think. It may very well be appropriate for you to do military service but not merely as a reflexive action based on family precedent.

Plainly speaking, the conundrum of the individual within society is that society is a congeries of individuals who enforce their individual interests and beliefs as societal interests and beliefs and, in enforcing their individual predilections as societal standards, conflate the two. Myths are created by persons injecting their present personal interests in their restating the past. Such deviation is an example of the mischief wreaked when persons fail to adhere to a sound model.

The calculation of self-interest is a practical problem worth everyone's introspection. Self-interest is commonly confused with the accumulation or concentration of power or wealth. But arrogance and greed limit the sustainable strength that may otherwise be achieved if persons were to recognize the positive and negative externalities of the concentration of self-interest. Although a person needs a modicum of power and wealth to avoid victimization by the vagaries of life, generosity of spirit and wealth in the dispersal of one's own power increases one's overall self-interest in gaining strength through diversity and countering the incentive of others to conspire against you. Although the gambit of self-sacrifice frequently goes unacknowledged, the long run sharing, rather than usurpation, of identity allows the emergence of the individual as a person unburdened from the tasks of hoarding social status and property. Self-interest is best found in the freedom of the spirit, liberation of the soul.

We are inherently social beings and to the extent that social accommodation of others does not suppress our own cusp of personality we should accommodate others. Society can enhance the overall level of well-being and happiness by providing or allowing geographical mobility, economic opportunity, general tolerance and fair elections. These conditions allow individuals to seek out and then inhabit the most comfortable social niche for themselves. Society in the end benefits.

Politics is the societal war between alternate realities with the battle lines being the seams of society. Good policy rests on well developed propositions of P-T-R. There are limits to how far enlightenment can go. Although change, sometimes labelled as enlightenment or progress, will occur, the change will be predominately in the relative degree of power as allegiances to identity congeries shift.

The bridge from society to your mind is populated with icons, sometimes in the form of ghosts. Another way of thinking about these residents of the mind is that our minds are co-extensive with the society we have experienced. In a sense, our minds are inhabited by the people with whom we have interacted although their ghosts may be superficially present in an abstract image. Masks are images of iconic personas that exist in niches of the mind. These personas are not whole, but emerge in various circumstances as uncluttered personifications of those partial personas. Lessons learned in the past and incorporated into the present can often be found to be attached to a person who in some way is the source of the lesson (the personification of abstract thought). A famous expression of the merger in the mind of persons and ghosts was the Ghost Dance performed by the Lakota Sioux in 1890 with a purpose of reuniting the living with their ancestors to resist the domination by the Federal Government and white settlers. Spirits and ghosts can control you but do not control external reality. They affect your understanding of external reality and your reaction to external reality as if the spirits and ghosts were in fact affecting the external reality. Shakespeare stated this proposition well in Henry the Fourth, part 1, act 3, scene 1:

"Glendower: I can call spirits from the vasty deep.

Hotspur (Percy):   Why, so can I, or so can any man; but will they come when you do call for them?"

"Possession" is simply the overwhelming of the psyche by one of the resident personalities and is an aberration of the mind. Excluding organic disease and other physiological problems, aberrations are merely extensions of the otherwise normal mind and the basic "normal" model of the mind is the starting point of all analysis. Hallucinations are dreams that are active while you are awake in contrast to delusions which are beliefs that are constructs of your point fixed events in your past. Delusions are erroneous assumptions stabilized in the ongoing development of your P-T-R structure while hallucinations are present sense perceptions created by the mind.

We all suffer the burdens of delusions and need to re-align our perceptions and articulations with reality but the nub of the problem is which reality? There is no escape from living a life controlled by the icons of your mind; icons that accumulate each day and are rudimentarily sorted at night as you rest, perchance to dream. Acceptance of a flawed and limited mind is the start to nighttime psychoanalysis in resolving dreams and early morning wakefulness. Anger and depression are indicators of creases in a person's internal logic. Resolving the problem of universal statements reduces the pain hammered by the superego. When a personality becomes fractured, the fault lines are between the different elements. Picture a person trying to piece Humpty-Dumpty back together by gluing shell fragments labelled P, T or R.

Analogous to the social architecture of society is the architecture of the mind. One solution to psychic pain and depression, at least for a brief period of time, is to relocate within your own mind the hub, your sense of identity, around which your thoughts revolve, to wit: a solution for an individual having difficulties with the "social order" is moving to a more accommodating room in the social architecture. Your most comfortable room in your mind's architecture is the room that you exercise the most power over your own mind. To the extent that you can control external events, your external control is referenced back to your own mental imagery. There is no external comfort; your psyche resides in your mind. Often more easily said than done but it can be done by active engagement with your own mind.

Can one find happiness within the mind's architecture? Can the meaning of events or memories be changed? Is one's reaction to the pain of overwhelming preoccupation to retreat into ignorance? To say, since I cannot master my fate, I absolve myself of responsibility for my acts and thoughts? To blend into the crowd? To accept what others believe? The dilemma for modern man as a social animal is to what extent an individual can define and live his own identity in contrast to the identities imposed upon him by society. Which raises the question of what cost are you willing to bear, what price you are willing to pay, in order to protect, preserve and enhance your cusp of personality? The treadmill lives that many people lead narrow their perspective and create the tunnel vision that blinds them to better, broader lives. To avoid the fate of a cog in a machine, one needs to seek balance in the expression of the elemental personas by diversification of interests and activities and undertake, what some people believe would be a vain attempt, to achieve the ability to see the reality of life and yet strive for the romance of life's potential for beauty, greatness and everyday good.

THE SOUTH PACIFIC

The exploration of the earth was simultaneously an exploration of the human psyche. The anthropological survey on great oceanic excursions plumbed the depths of who we are and what distinguishes our own identities in the grand view of society. We accept and even embrace symbols, such as tattoos the art of which Europeans learned from the Maori and perhaps other South Pacific peoples, because we lack power over our existence. Symbols constitute a substitute for power. Through symbols, our minds enter fantasy worlds in which we are no longer weak buffeted about by forces beyond our control but are strong, free to pursue a vision of life that reaffirms our sense of identity. The dynamics and politics of identity (T) are writ large in the history of the relationship between Europeans and Native North Americans. Vine Deloria, Jr., in his books such as Custer Died for Your Sins (1969) and We Talk, You Listen (1970), may be the best guide for those who are unfamiliar with that history. Analogous (but with significant differences) histories are found in the interaction of English migrants and the Bush People of Australia as well as the eastward migration of European Russians. The history of slavery is different in that while identity was used as a badge the predominant logic was power rather than identity. Resources, ethnicity, historical claims, etc. are all superficial causes of war; superficial because they all exist even in the absence of war. What distinguishes war is the compulsion to act; compulsion is an emotional state of mind and not an external set of events.

Discretionary decisions to instigate war ultimately rest on the mind set of leaders with the power to implement the decision to wage war. Discretionary wars are not based on national interests but illusions of grandeur promulgated by ruling cliques. "History repeats itself" not because leaders are ignorant of history but because the implementing mindset naturally arises spontaneously out of the statistical distribution of P-T-R combinations. Discretionary war is simply the grossest example of the inevitability of irrationality which permeates our entire lives having arisen in the process of development of the psyche in our individual lives. We can not escape it but we can confront it to emerge, not unscathed, but better in all aspects of our lives. War, once it goes beyond ritualistic displays, is beyond mere "tribalism" and marginal adjustments in the social order. The social order is within our ken but war is beyond our ordinary understanding. War is an act of compulsion and the elements of compulsion are the roots of war. In life, and in particular war, how do you know who your enemy is? Sure, there are many glib, simplistic answers that would win over an audience in a public debate but those quips do not solve the very real epistemological problem that underlie wars such as Lyndon Johnson's Viet Nam War. It is abundantly clear now what many observers thought then: that the United States military and diplomatic corps did not have a sound epistemological understanding of the United States' undertaking of responsibility for Southeast Asia. Daniel Ellsberg, who is most famous for his releasing to the press the presumably confidential Department of Defense history of the Viet Nam War popularly known as The Pentagon Papers, had originally been during his tour of duty in Viet Nam an enthusiastic believer in the American military excursion into Viet Nam. He subsequently converted, while employed by the Rand Corporation, to pacifism with the aid of a muse while attending a conference in Princeton, New Jersey. Prior to his service in Viet Nam, Daniel Ellsberg as a graduate student studied the Maori conquest of the Chatham Islanders. In December, 1835, Maori warriors from New Zealand sailed an extraordinary distance to the Chatham Islands to conquer the inhabitants of the Chatham Islands. Prior to being told by Europeans of the existence of the Chatham Islanders, the Maori were completely unaware that the Chatham Islanders existed and it is clear that the Chatham Islanders posed no threat of any sort to the Maori people. See Jared Diamond, Guns, Germs and Steel (1997) pp. 53-57.

JURY DELIBERATIONS

Jury deliberations provide a demonstration that truth seeking is not a mechanical process. Since court rules and practices vary among the jurisdictions and the nature of the case being considered, the following comments should not be interpreted as universal but should nonetheless be instructive.

In a criminal law case being tried in the State of New York, the jury is instructed orally by the judge and is not provided with a written set of jury instructions or the indictment. The jury is provided with a verdict sheet and is allowed to examine the exhibits. In addition, the jury may ask for oral read-backs of testimony but would not be given a written transcript.

I believe that the conventional understanding as to why a jury should not be given written instructions in addition to the oral instructions is to prevent jurors from selectively reading portions and ignoring other related instructions. In a jury's request for clarification, the judge will presumably accurately restate the relevant (and perhaps interrelated) instructions, typically saying exactly what the judge originally said to the jury.

As to the indictment, that is not evidence and the charges are provided to the jury through the judge's oral instructions to the jury.

The significance of oral instruction is that it forces lay people to understand in their own minds the case before them. There is a difference in reasoning between being given a written set of standards and then matching evidence with the standards (which is essentially a mechanical process in which the person does not need to understand either the standard or the corresponding evidence) and being orally instructed which requires the juror to at least incorporate into the juror's thinking, whether or not the juror actually understands, the standards through which the juror is to deliberate. Thus, we come to judgment being the basis for truth, the verdict, which of course may be in error.

It so happens that the proposition that computers could replace jurors to determine judicial trial outcomes has its roots in the compilation of the law of evidence by John Henry Wigmore. He published the first version of the standard treatise on evidence (A Treatise on the System of Evidence in Trials at Common Law) in 1904. There have been many updated versions of Wigmore on Evidence over the intervening decades with recent editions readily available. "Wigmore on Evidence" presents the conventional understanding of the law of judicial evidence.

Wigmore conceived, under the rubric of "The Problem of Proof", of an alternative theory of evidence and trial based on probability and belief. His theory was eventually applied in an analysis of the Sacco & Venzetti case, a cause celebre with a voluminous literature reflecting its social significance. Joseph B. Kahane and David A. Schum used Wigmore's alternative theory of evidence in doing their probability analysis of the evidence in the Sacco & Venzetti case. My own view is that a Wigmore chart gets you only so far and never reaches the ultimate question.

THE TEST

My most compelling factor in the way I have lived my life and the source of many of my failures is my inclination towards rationality as a unifying principle. I pushed unification theory too far in practice and was flummoxed when it was not accepted in implementation in various cells of society, including such fractals as the courts of law. Unification theory lies buried beneath the middens of reaction rather than thought.

One of the great tragedies in our lives is the tendency to typecast intelligence too early and not allow the emergence of one's abilities in endeavors that would earlier seem out of reach. There is no single standard of intelligence. One can be extraordinarily intelligent in some mental task but inept in many others. Examples of this phenomenon can be found among the chess grandmasters, e.g. Bobby Fischer. Part of the problem with "highly intelligent" people is that they are so taken with their supposed intelligence that they are deaf and blind to ordinary life. Having cast the die too soon, they fail to diversify their interests and endeavors and, thus, become relegated to the realm of short hitters who stay at home rather than go over the wall to venture beyond their horizons. What is even worse than self-imposed limitations is the enforcement by others of what they perceive to be a person's limitations.

Elemental analysis, being a universal (and not a partial) philosophy, is subject to a myriad of tests, whether by logicians, psychiatrists or medical researchers investigating human ontogeny. Each investigator will reach his own conclusion that may refute or confirm a part of elemental analysis.

The test, in the end, is not whether I have proved the truth of every component of this theory. The test is whether you in your own way can implement these ideas into meaningful beliefs and actions. Even if there is some fundamental flaw in my concept so that it is ultimately partial rather than universal, there is some utility in its technique as a parsing tool for thoughts and statements. Perhaps consider this philosophy as a lens that allows you to see more clearly than you would otherwise.

Q. E. D.

I HAVE SOLVED the equation.

A major theme in my general thesis that all human endeavors are susceptible to elemental analysis is the specific theme that wars and battles are also so analyzable. One of the practical problems in doing elemental analysis of a war or battle is that the task becomes overwhelming by the paradox of having a super-abundance of information combined with the ignorance generated by the fog of war.

Because of the peculiar combination of a relatively well defined scope of definition and the manageable records of the event, the Battle of the Little Bighorn (Battle of the Greasy Grass; Custer's Last Stand) that occurred on June 25 & 26, 1876, between a coalition of Native Americans encamped along the Little Bighorn River in Montana and attacking units of the United States Army is an excellent candidate for a detailed elemental analysis by a scholar seeking to apply my methodology.

A key concept to such an analysis would be the development of a time line of perceptions by various persons including those close to but not present in the field of battle. What was believed and what was known become central in a perception based analysis toward an understanding of how the battle came to be, which in retrospect the Native Americans would have preferred to have avoided and the United States Army would have preferred not to have instigated.

To answer the question I posed at the beginning of this quest, I respond to fathers who would, somewhat In the manner of Tantalus, send their sons into wars that cannot be won that their duty, as fathers, is not to crush their sons' souls but to liberate their spirits. A hallmark of a civilized person is the ability to control one's beliefs rather than being enslaved to what the person may think he understands but in fact does not.

My inquiry, this reasonable adventure, is the pursuit of the sun as it disappears beneath the western horizon having illuminated the days of our lives. What happened we may know but who, other than sleepwalkers, would not want another hour, another two hours of illumination?

Matti Bucca and Villi Boca, as you walk with me in the autumn woods of my life, it will come time for my winter's sleep, a sleep of contentment. I will go gentle into that good night. Do not rage against the dying light. I have guided you out of the labyrinth this far, the trail continues for you, go on without me, a new world awaits.

Joy! Joy!! Joy!!! ….

Pax vobiscum.
Dad

END NOTES

These end notes provide a reader's guide for names and concepts so that you may follow my argument without the distraction of consulting outside materials except those that you choose to pursue for greater understanding.

DEDICATION

One of John Ferguson's kindnesses to me was to allow me to deviate from his course's syllabus by his suggesting that I read Robert Ardrey's *African Genesis* (1961) in substitution for part of the syllabus. What is obvious in retrospect is that Shakespeare's plays are the merger of psychology and language. Although these plays are assigned to the English curriculum as steps in mastering the English language, the psychology is preeminent and beyond the ken of the common adolescent mind.

John Ferguson was one of the selectors of Jacob Bronowski's *Science and Human Values* (1956) for school-wide discussion outside the prescribed, standard curriculum at The Mercersburg Academy. As an aside here, I believe that Bronowski's thesis in *Science and Human Values* is flawed as based on a dualistic rather than tri-partite mind but, in being so flawed, is not otherwise necessarily in error.

Compare Freud's life instinct (eros) and death instinct (thanatos) with Gandhi's unity of life (ahimsa) and destruction of life (himsa). See part 4 section XXXIX "A Spiritual Dilemma" in Gandhi's autobiography in which section Gandhi discusses the relevance of ahimsa to service in war. Query whether eros and thanatos are reflected in the odds of truthful communication. See the section The Probability of Truthful Statements, supra. To wit: eros being reflected in the minor set for corresponding elements in transmission and reception; thanatos being reflected in the major set of discordant communication.

One of the earliest philosophical questions from antiquity was "How many principles do we need to explain the natural world?" This question is ambiguous for there is a difference between explaining the natural world and the actual operation of nature itself. As should be abundantly evident in this extended essay, I believe that explanation can be reduced to three principles. However, the operation of nature, and the universe for that matter, is not dependent on explanation. Thus, I do not propound that nature and the universe operate ultimately on three principles.

I discuss the working of the mind but do not mean to imply that the mind exists outside of the body within which it resides. The host body is subject to a vast array of phenomena. Ohashi in his Reading the Body (1991) maintains that: "In Eastern philosophy, the body is seen as an orchestra whose music is the soul. Remove any instrument, or change the way it is played, and you alter the music entirely. To bring out the full breadth of the spirit, you must finely tune each organ as if it were an instrument. And each organ must blend harmoniously with the rest of the body...."

My unification theory is in part an attempt to reconcile two of the most abstract and distinct theories of thought of the East (Zen Buddhism} and the West (Freudian Analysis). Rudyard Kipling opined that "East is East, and West is West, and never the twain shall meet...." (The Ballad of East and West, 1889).

The big lesson of anthropology is that, although humans are highly adaptable and have a surplus of intelligence, all humans need to organize their thoughts as well as their societies and that organization starts with an assertion.

HOW TO READ THE SYMPHONY OF THE MIND

"...the study of philosophy...is the noblest and best of music." Socrates in Plato's Phaedo (translation by Benjamin Jowett).

"White paper" refers to a specific type of policy writing originating in Britain in the Twentieth Century.

Step by Step alludes to Step by Step: political writings — 1936-1939 by Winston S. Churchill (1939).

One of the skills needed to study law and to practice law in an intelligent manner is "issue spotting." "Issues" are what lead to analysis. E.g., the IRAC law school mantra (issue, rule, application and conclusion). Analogous situations in life arise in all sorts of endeavors. The point is that to "miss an issue" is to be blind to an opportunity. When you "screw up," analyze why you missed recognizing the operative issue.

Robert M. Pirsig, Zen and the Art of Motorcycle Maintenance: an inquiry into values (1974). See also Ronald L. DiSanto and Thomas J. Steele, Guidebook to Zen and the Art of Motorcycle Maintenance (1990). As a matter secondary to my father and son investigation, elemental analysis is my response to Robert Pirsig's inquiry into values, in particular "quality." He was, of course, correct in asserting that "quality" is a fundamental question. Compare quality with "more" (quantity) regarding what you seek to gain out of your life.

To step aside from the abstract for a moment, the concept of "quality" in food is explored by Jimmy LeSage in his Forty Years of Authentic Wellness (2017). My views are partially informed by conversations I had with Jimmy LeSage at Mendon, Vermont, during September, 2017. Jimmy LeSage's views are in accord with those of Henri Charpentier. "In your kitchen a good quality of food, rather than a great quantity, should prevail." Henri Charpentier, The Henri Charpentier Cookbook (1945, 1970), p. 31. I have been hesitant to include the Charpentier quote because I fear that some readers will find its inclusion as a basis to ridicule this essay in that they may see it as analogous to the dicta of Chance, the gardener, in Jerzy Kosinski's Being There (1970) (which may have been derived from Tadeusz Dolega-Mostowicz's Kariera Nikodema Dyzmy - 1932). Even Marcus Aurelius is vulnerable to Chance-the-gardener ridicule. See, e.g., the passage in Book XI of Meditations regarding pruning and grafting. However, if one is to truly understand Homo sapiens, then one must include all that pertains to Homo sapiens in one's analysis. Questions of elective diet go well beyond gustibus as taste is another pathway into the mind. Ayurveda, a traditional system of Hindu medicine, states "that each of us has a different combination of the three doshas or types — kapha, vata and pitta — that create our unique mental and physical characteristics, and which need to be balanced for optimum health and happiness. Most of us have one or two doshas that are most active, and Ayurveda seeks to redress this imbalance, primarily through diet." Pushpesh Pant, India Cookbook p.10 (2010). "There is compelling evidence to show that there is a relationship between the quality of your diet and your mental health. This relationship goes beyond the effect of diet on your body size or other aspects of health that can in turn affect your mood." Camille Lassale quoted by Nina Avramova in CNN article (09/26/2018) "Mediterranean Diet Could Prevent Depression." See Camille Lassale, G. David Batty, Amaria Baghdadli, Feliece Jacka, Almudena Sanchez-Villegas, Mika Kivimaki & Tasnime Akbaraly, Healthy dietary indices and risk of depressive outcomes: a systematic review and meta-analysis of observational studies, Molecular Psychiatry (2018).

Jean Larteguy in his novel The Centurions (1960, 1961) discusses (at pp. 190 & 191) the "re-education " of POWs and the role of diet, specifically the daily caloric intake, as the attempt to use the stomach [via blood sugar levels to influence the mind by its sense of hunger] as a doorway into the mind of a POW.

Quality is certainly an important concept for organizing and conducting one's life. An element to leading a quality life is to elect complexity and diversity of interests and activities. This election provides stability to one's psyche by reducing its vulnerability to fortune (fortuna) or conditions changing adversely in the environment of a simple life.

"Autobiography" as used here is a riddle. The solution of which is that I am discussing my own mind over four decades of adult introspection.

Although I know little about Sigmund Freud and even less about Ludwig Wittgenstein, my thesis is on one level a Freudian interpretation of Wittgenstein's Tractatus Logico-Philosophicus (1921) as a letter to my sons being a comprehensible tractatus philosophical. If you are intrigued by Wittgenstein's over-arching proposition, you may want to compare John Fowles' The Aristos: a self-portrait of ideas (1964).

FIRST PREFACE

Marcel Proust, Swann's Way (also known as: Remembrance of Things Past), 1913. In a subsequent passage, Proust provides an exegesis.

SECOND PREFACE

Charles Driscoll, Esq., told me this Balls and Strikes joke at a New Year's Day party hosted by Stephen Sprague, Esq., in Albuquerque in the early '80s. A published version of the joke is in Ronald P. Sokol's Justice after Darwin (1975); see pp. 52-53 regarding Prof. F. D. G. Riddle's use of the umpire joke to illustrate three different theories of law.

THIRD PREFACE

Buddhist practice postulates OM as the reduction of all knowledge to its most succinct form.

OM is a sound produced as a meditative practice.

What did the world sound like before there was complex music? As Leslie Conover mentioned to me, complex music arose through the development of technology such as the piano. To make the point more obvious, there were no symphonic concerts conducted in ancient Greece. It is difficult to comprehend how an ancient Greek composer could in the abstract design what would be the equivalent of George Frideric Handel's Messiah (1741). What does the rise of complex music tell us about the mind?

Music existed prior to its rise in human created sound. The complex vocalizations of cetaceans seem to go beyond the mere signaling of bird song. A few birds, such as ravens, are capable of conversations beyond signaling.

Query: Can music analysis be a pathway to understanding the mind's internal logic? Stephen Johnson suggests so in his discussion of composer Dmitri Shostakovich's music. "I sensed the glimmering of a possibility. If Shostakovich could find the 'method', the thread of logic, in his teeming, cascading thoughts, then perhaps I could too." See Stephen Johnson, How Shostakovich Changed My Mind (2019).

Analogous to the question of the evolution of the mind through sound as a function of the development of music technology is the question of the evolution of the mind through the senses of smell, taste and feel. The basic force was trade through world travel such as the Silk Road and the rise of maritime shipping. Of course the trading involved the flow of goods in both directions between East and West and not just the payment in gold and silver. An example worth contemplating is the enhancement of Asian Indian cuisine by the importation of chile (chili) peppers from the Americas. Query: Does the introduction of variety in the diet enhance or stimulate the mind? Is diet another door of perception and another entrance to understanding the mind?

The senses of sight, hearing, smell, taste and touch provide "inputs" (information signals) to the mind which processes the signals. See Preface I re Proust's "Petites Madeleines," supra. It is this processing of inputs, in addition to the endogenous self-sustaining cusp of personality, that must be accounted for in any comprehensive and unified model of the mind.

FOURTH PREFACE

Perhaps an echo of Rod Serling's introductions to episodes of The Twilight Zone (television series, 1959-1964).

FIFTH PREFACE

W. B. Yeats' The Second Coming (1919) can be parsed to whatever level of understanding you care to reach.

SIXTH PREFACE

The cinema version of Michael Lewis' book The Big Short (2010) is a richly intertwined depiction of the psychology of business transactions. The Big Short screenplay by Charles Randolph and Adam McKay (based upon the book by Michael Lewis) (Buff Revised, May 11, 2015).

Downloadable full versions of many produced screenplays are available at no cost "on the internet." Begin your search generically for screenplays and then look for the particular screenplay that interests you. Many screenplays are fast productive reads.

Listening is a form of looking.

SEVENTH PREFACE

Compare the three Fates (Clotho, Lachesis and Atropos) of Greek mythology as well as the three Norns (Urd, Verdandi and Skuld) of Norse mythology. Are the Witches of Macbeth derived from the Norns and are the Norns derived from the Fates? Or do they independently arise in Greek, Norse and British cultures?

INTRODUCTION

Matti Bucca and Villi Boca: Finnish names of love given by Liisa and me to our sons in their infancy.

An analogous query was addressed by Ivan Turgenev in his Fathers and Sons (1862).

Although the Viet Nam War could be characterized in an end note, such a brief statement would be misleading as to the rich complexity of the impact it had on American society. To familiarize yourself with this geopolitical excursion, you might start with The Pentagon Papers (available in many forms of publication), Stanley Karnow's Vietnam: a history (1983) and Frances Fitzgerald's Fire in the Lake (1972). A central question of the Viet Nam War is President Lyndon Johnson's decision to escalate America's military presence after campaigning in 1964 as the peace candidate vis-a-vis Senator Barry Goldwater. (See the "Daisy" ad from that campaign. September 7, 1964, NBC). The conventional analysis of LBJ's motivation was the hand-in-glove combination of a belief in geo-political commitments and the attempt to avoid being blamed for the "loss of Viet Nam" to Communism in the vein of the blame following the fall of China to Communism following WWII. However, an alternative premise for LBJ's motivation to escalate was as an attempt to regain the support of the Southern States for his Democratic administration after the passage of the Civil Rights Act of 1964. LBJ may have felt, as a matter of shrewd political calculation, that the militarism of the South would cause the South to support his Democratic administration in conducting a war rather than turn to the Republican Party.

The contemporaneous accounts of the United States' excursion into Southeast Asia were frequent and across the full range of media expressing a full spectrum of perspectives. In light of the pathetic failure of that excursion, it is important to know that it is easy now to emphasize the contemporaneous criticisms and ignore the acceptance of the war by many Americans. For a saccharine account directed at the general American public, see Peter T. White and Winfield Parks, Behind the Headlines in Viet Nam, National Geographic (vol. 131, #2, pp. 149-193) published in February, 1967. Compare the retrospective survey (Vietnam as the Past) that appeared in the Summer 1983 issue of The Wilson Quarterly (vol. VII, #3, pp. 94-139). To obtain a taste of the domestic turmoil of the Sixties, see Norman Mailer's The Armies of the Night: the novel as history / history as a novel (1968).

War is generally discussed in semi-abstract terms that gloss over the horrors in the conduct of military operations. Sometimes legalisms are used to side step the personal responsibility for one's own actions (e.g., homicide in battle is "justified" and therefore is not murder). Other logics use "group think" or "us versus them" to justify the horrors of battle. It is particularly easy for persons who have not been directly involved in combat to gloss over the psychological costs of combat.

Military actions are not neat implementations of national policy translated through some calculus of force applied against the enemy's resistance to have its will subdued. War and combat are theaters that invite the emergence of the worst of human nature.

Aside from the horrors of war that are contemplated in policy (such as the United States' fire bombing of Tokyo and the atomic bombing of Hiroshima and Nagasaki (see, e.g., John Hershey, Hiroshima [1946]), the emergence of private murder, opportunistic pillaging, and epidemic rape in theatres of war is commonplace. In some instances, the feral hogs of war are condoned as implements of policy. Examples are the Japanese rape of Nanking (1937), Soviet troops brutalizing civilians in Eastern Europe (1945), and the abducting of girls in Central Africa in recent years.

War itself is bad enough but these atrocities challenge the capabilities of soldiers to resist being sucked into the morass of group conformity. There can be no chivalry in sending boys into harm's way.

It is all too easy to not grasp the horror of war when the atrocities are inflicted in a foreign country. It is silly to accept the McNamarization of war that conflates metrics with reality. Metrics failed in Viet Nam; reality won. Jean Larteguy at p. 188 in The Centurions, provides a succinct explanation in comparing the 32 card game of belote with 52 card bridge regarding the French-Vietminh War of why Sparta won the Peloponnesian War against Athens but Athens prevailing in the long run.

Soldiers' individual experiences in war vary widely according to their degrees of exposure to combat. Being in the zone of engagement converts metrics to the personal and ignorance into soul shaping wrestling with horror. For a detailed example of such human debasement, see Daniel Lang's Casualties of War, The New Yorker (October 18, 1969).

Two of the basic components in the fathers' belief that their sons should go off to a war that cannot be won is the conflating of the fathers' prior service in a "just war" with their sons' service in a "nonsense war" as well as the fathers' avoiding embarrassment in the fathers' perceived community and the community's elements of peer bonding and the resulting group thinking. Query what difference it makes as to which community the fathers believe that they belong. In re fathers' complicity of sending sons to Viet Nam, consider Abraham's dilemma as to whether to sacrifice his son Isaac. Genesis: 22; Koran 37:100-113. Similarly in a Greek myth, Tantalus had difficulty understanding how to please his gods. In an attempt to curry favor with them, Tantalus cooked his son and served him at a banquet for Tantalus' gods. Tantalus ended up by bobbing up and down in a water well with grapes just out of his reach. Fathers think they know much more than they actually understand. Marcus Aurelius in Book XII of his Meditations observed: "I have often wondered how it is that every man loves himself more than all the rest of men, but yet sets less value on his own opinion of himself than on the opinion of others. ... So it is clear that we accord much more respect to what our neighbors think of us than to what we think of ourselves." Earlier in Book VIII, he counsels "If then you have truly seen where the matter lies, throw away the thought of how you might seem to others, and be content if you live the rest of your life in the manner that your nature wills."

"If any question why we died: Tell them, because our fathers lied." Rudyard Kipling, Epitaphs of War (1914-18). Kipling's son, John Kipling, was at the age of 16 medically rejected twice for military service. Rudyard Kipling interceded and, as a result, John Kipling was commissioned into the Irish Guards two days short of his 17th birthday. About a month after his 18th birthday, John Kipling was killed at the Battle of Loos.

Titanic is used here both in the ordinary sense of describing the scale of forces as well as the metaphor of the "unsinkable" ship sinking on its maiden voyage. Serendipitously, the term also references Freudian psychology that is evident in another dysfunctional father-son relationship found in the struggles between fathers and sons among the Titans in Roman mythology. In Roman mythology as derived from Greek mythology, Saturn, who had overthrown his father Uranus, ate his children to forestall being overthrown by one of them. Saturn's wife hid their sixth child, Jupiter, who eventually overthrew Saturn. Franciso Goya depicted Saturn Devouring His Son (Saturno devorando a su hijo) as one of his Black Paintings (Pinturas Negras) (1819-1823).

Optimum optimorum is the philosophical concept of an unambiguous unified maximization of human well-being. It can not exist except in the minds of zealots and science fiction writers. Less rigorous and more practical alternatives are the "greatest good for the greatest number" (Italian) and the "greatest good of the greatest number in the long run" (American Progressive).

Gordian Knots exist as physical objects and, as physical objects, their unraveling (the solving of the problem) is quite ordinary. Alexander's resorting to a sword to cut the knot is, in my view, an apocryphal metaphor for the use of power to "solve" otherwise intractable problems. Once a hierarchy is imposed, the subsidiary issues fall into place. Buddhism has an analogous personage in Achala (Manjushri), as a god of knowledge, who is often depicted with a sword in his right hand. Contrast the methodology of "cutting" the knot with the Freudian methodology of "unweaving" the knot. The results are quite different: Alexander's trading one power structure for another and Freud's resolution of the conflicts within a power structure.

Alexander the Great (356-323 B.C.), as king of Macedonia, created an empire by military conquest in what is now known as the Middle East.

Stella Adler, Stella Adler on America's Master Playwrights (Alfred A. Knopf, New York, 2012).

See the work of Abraham Maslow, such as Toward a Psychology of Being (1962, 1968). Maslow seems to have implied that "peak experiences" are positive events, but I believe that negative events can coalesce into a peak experience. Daniel Ellsberg was a true believer during the time that he served as a Marine in Viet Nam and his psyche at the time fed off the icons of war. Of course, his reasoning ability later gave rise to a change in his understanding of himself and the war. But, at the time, he relished his involvement in the combat zone. Inherent natural logical induction and the ordinary processes of life failed to provide an encompassing, accurate perception of evil.

In a sermon given on March 24, 1980, Salvadoran Archbishop Oscar Romero said: "I would like to make a special appeal to the men of the army, and specifically to the ranks of the National Guard, the police and the military. Brothers, you come from our own people. You are killing your own brother peasants when any human order to kill must be subordinate to the law of God which says, 'Thou shall not kill.' … In the name of God, in the name of this suffering people whose cries rise to heaven more loudly each day, I implore you, I beg you, I order you in the name of God: Stop the repression." The next day, March 25, 1980, Archbishop Romero was assassinated.

Roy Heath, The Reasonable Adventurer (1964).

Marcus Aurelius in Book XI of his Meditations states: "These are the properties of the rational soul: it sees itself, analyzes itself, makes itself such as it chooses, itself reaps its own fruits…. … …it makes what has been set before it full and complete, so that it can say, 'I have what is my own.'"

David Thoreau, Resistance to Civil Government (a/k/a On the Duty of Civil Disobedience) (1849).

Mohandras Gandhi (1869-1948) led the civil disobedience resistance against British colonial rule in India. He was assassinated on January 30, 1948, by a Hindu nationalist following the partition in 1947 of the South Asian subcontinent into what then became India and Pakistan. Gandhi was one of the great political leaders who eschewed identity politics and he had attempted to avoid the division of religions into separate nations.

My dissertation purports to be philosophical. Philosophy has been taught in many guises but I argue that philosophy is ultimately psychological, a product of the mind. To revisit, for example Socrates, his great issues and methodology largely resolve themselves if one interprets the life and dialogues of Socrates as projections of his personality rather than intellect. Socrates accepted hemlock on a personal basis, not as a result of any assumed correctness of the sentence. He was disliked by the ruling coterie not because of his beliefs but because who he was as a persona. He was charged with "corrupting young men and introducing new gods." At least the part of "introducing new gods" is a reference to the teaching of unconventional, i.e. non-conforming, ways of thinking. Thus, Socrates can be viewed as a patron of individualism.

A succinct poetic critique of political discourse is found in Boethius' Consolation of Philosophy (Book One, Part III) wherein Boethius' muse Philosophy states: "...Socrates was unjustly put to death — a victorious death won with me at his side. After that the mobs of Epicureans and Stoics and the others each did all they could to seize for themselves the inheritance of wisdom that he left. As part of their plunder they tried to carry me off, but I fought and struggled, and in the fight the robe was torn which I had woven with my own hands. They tore off little pieces from it and went away in the fond belief that they had obtained the whole of philosophy. The sight of traces of my clothing on them gained them the reputation among the ignorant of being my familiars, and as a result many of them became corrupted by the ignorance of the uninitiated mob."

The predominant force in society is conformity. People do not think; they conform. Non-conformists are excluded as a matter of course. Joseph Campbell, a scholar of mythology whose most famous thesis is that of "the hero's journey", considered himself a maverick in his propounding the interface of the individual and society. Conformists expect, insist and enforce their expectation that non-conformists conform. In a social asymmetry, non-conformists are more willing to accommodate the conformists than the conformists, who perhaps are incapable even if they were willing, to accommodate the non-conformists. Philosophers, as well as those who are so inclined, as opposed to apologists, do not do well in bureaucracies (e.g., Aldo Leopold and his final assignment in the United States Forest Service as deputy administrator of the USFS Forest Products Laboratory). Apologists, such as Edwin Teller, on the other hand, not only survive but even thrive (compare the career arcs of Edwin Teller and J. Robert Oppenheimer). Intellectual honesty led to the termination of the career of diplomat John Paton Davies as a "China Hand" as the mid-Twentieth Century Cold War emerged. In the long run honest accurate perceptions are best but the coin of politics is stamped with Speaker of the House Sam Rayburn's dictum: "If you want to get along, go along."

The perversity of office politics was parodied in the comic opera H.M.S. Pinafore by Gilbert & Sullivan, particularly the song "When I Was a Lad" in Act I (1878). Although careers based on office politics are, and always have been, commonplace, "When I Was a Lad" richly foretold the political career of Dick Cheney, a neo-con hawk who actively avoided military service of his own.

Query: Who had a better grasp of truth and reality—the pariah I. F. "Izzy" Stone, editor and publisher of I. F. Stone's Weekly which was a gadfly critique of the United States' Viet Nam War policy, or Robert "Whiz Kid" McNamara, the Secretary Defense who "managed" that war in great detail but with little insight or understanding?

I see philosophy as method with the focus being rather narrow except that the method must be universally applicable. There are other forms of philosophy: comprehensive in the style of Plato and Freud; cataloging or encyclopedic as with Bertrand Russell; and selective such as Socrates. In the rough-and-tumble of personal and political argument, an asserted philosophy, perhaps in a State Department white paper, may be no more than the patina on the brass of a decision.

FREUDIAN DOCTRINE

Sigmund Freud (1856-1939) was perhaps unique as a person who had a unified and objective understanding of society by means to view the madness with both breadth and acuity. My own understanding of Freudian theory has been in part informed by decades of conversations with my late brother Wendell Kury, a board certified psychiatrist.

Over the years, Freud has had many detractors, such as Frederick Crews (Freud: the making of an illusion — 2017). See also Gene Lyons' essay "Psychology's theories Don't Always Stand the Test of Time" (2019). Freud's writings and teachings are subject to analytical criticism. However, the core model is valid. By and large, the detractors are like people looking for gold in a gold mill's tailings rather than in the mill's pay out pan.

For a social history of psychoanalysis, see Eli Zaretsky's Secrets of the Soul: a social and cultural history of psychoanalysis (2004).

Freud's writings are voluminous and discursive. To master them is to master the arcane, by which the mastery of the details and scholarly historical correctness obscure the functional understanding of a truly elegant model. Jung forsook adherence to the intellectual rigor embraced by Freud and propounded a mystical reinterpretation that is more easily learned and is, thus, more accessible to those who inquire. Jungian psychology is also more accepting than Freudian psychology of religions and might be a better way to access religious systems. See, e.g., Rob Preece's The Psychology of Buddhist Tantra (2000, 2006). However, Freud correctly interpreted religion as an artifact of the mind.

Freudian therapy is based, at least in part, on the proposition that the exegesis of a trauma leads to a resolution such that the trauma is no longer controlling or painful. In Zen Buddhism, the analogy is along the lines of: "When false discrimination stirs, experience it. If this experience of birth and death is not learned or practiced in the style of discrimination and there is no attachment to it, then each thought will be immediately liberated." See S. van Schaik's Tibetan Zen: discovering a lost tradition pp. 124, 135-136 (2015).

Freudian psychology and Zen Buddhism both have a method and a map with comparable levels of resolution. Their respective methods, while developed, are nonetheless obscure compared with the seeming clarity of their maps composed of their vast, and sometimes incomprehensible, respective literatures. These maps are inadequate by themselves.

Freudian and Zen literature are overflowing with arcana, in which the profit of distilling is negligible. Both are best applied with their respective core methods and an open mind devoid of doctrine. Doctrine nullifies analysis; analysis is the way and doctrine is the obstacle. Always reject doctrine; go with analysis.

Freud suggested that pain and compulsive behaviors disappear upon the resolution of the underlying trauma. I do not believe that resolution works so magically; the trauma reactions continue but are more manageable and less debilitating. Psychological pain can be largely resolved once you implement the realization that you and everyone else (including most importantly the people with whom you interact) live at least three lives simultaneously.

The reason that Freudian analysis does not work magically in relieving mental dysfunction (i.e., realization leading to immediate resolution) is that the realization occurring in analysis (whether self or otherwise) is simply an incomplete statement that serves as a transfer station between a carousel and a Ferris wheel. Reasoning is a bird's nest of loops rather than a set of equivalences.

Pain, particularly ancient pain, re-emerges in your dreams and nighttime wakefulness, often as you are about to rise for the coming day. The pain can be quite acute because in sleep your body is defenseless and has no power to confront the unresolved conflict. The mind is aware of the body's state of repose. You are in a sense "spinning your wheels" with no traction to move forward beyond that frozen point in time. The acute pain of early morning, when a person is most vulnerable and is least able to do any thing constructive to remedy the dilemma, gives rise to solitary suicides. A famous example is that of Ernest Hemingway who killed himself at 7:30 a.m. (July 2, 1961).

Early morning pain can be an impetus for productivity if one attempts to resolve the beleaguering conflicts by acting, in Shakespeare's words, "to take Arms against a Sea of troubles, And by opposing end them" thereby defeating rather than just suffering "The slings and arrows of outrageous fortune." Hamlet, Act III, Scene 1.

Having awaken in the middle of the night, then to be driven from bed by the hectoring of the demons of the pre-dawn howling like monkeys in the verbal jungle of the Panamanian rain forest, I went through my early morning rituals and then began to compose as best I could those thoughts I thought most useful to getting on with life; if you will: a guide to the world of demons that wreck havoc with our souls like harpy eagles in the rain forest snatching monkeys as the monkeys are eating fruit in the sunny crowns of tropical trees.

Query: Do howling monkeys have nightmares? If so, are nightmares a partial explanation of the timing of the dawn cacophony along with defense of territory, emerging light and endogenous self sustaining oscillators? In other words, do abstract demons exist in howling monkeys' minds? If howling monkeys have nightmares about territorial conflict with neighboring troops of howling monkeys, do they also have nightmares about their troop being preyed upon by harpy eagles? Could a mother howler have a nightmare following the grabbing of her infant by a harpy? Could a troop member have a nightmare following the grabbing of a friend by a harpy?

Regarding howling monkeys, see C. R. Carpenter, "Behavior and Social Relations of the Howling Monkey, " Comparative Psychology Monographs, John Hopkins University (May, 1934).

Dreams are the dynamic equivalent of perceptions of reality in that the mind deconstructs a perception into its component elements and translates those elements into a different image ala a rotating kaleidoscope in an attempt to resolve the frustration and tension present in the original perception.

Pain that can be confronted is manageable. Many years ago, a Viet Nam veteran who was assigned helicopter duty told me that, when he was working on a medical evacuation helicopter that was taking rounds, he was scared "shitless." After he was re-assigned to duties on a helicopter gunship, he felt much better.

There has existed (primarily when Freudian analysis was au courant) an oneiric school of cinema interpretation, which interpreted cinema as dreams subject to Freudian analysis, with Freud's Interpretation of Dreams serving as a manual. While cinema as well as all other human endeavors are subject to elemental analysis, whether any particular movie can be deeply analyzed as a "dream" may reflect more whimsy than the reality of how movies are created and produced. While all cinema (as well as all knowledge) is a variation of the P-T-R theme, the human dilemma that I am exegeting or parsing here is comically depicted in The Zero Theorem (2013). Similarly, see Darren Aronofsky's Pi (1998). Jumanji (1995) is comedic cinematic depiction of the mind.

Inception (2010), a sci-fi psychological thriller that I find comedic, presents a model of the mind that cobbles together the palace of memories with almost instantaneous situation shifting along with the layers of the mind increasing exponentially in memory data. Being a motion picture for a general audience, certain cinematic conventions were utilized such as an overblown chase sequence founded famously in The French Connection (cinema, 1971) and obligatory in the James Bond movies. Chase scenes do occur in real dreams but in a more elemental less cinematic way.

That cells can create an apparently seamless unified image of reality is demonstrated by Stanley Kubrick's Overlook Hotel in the movie The Shining (1980) being composed of several locations shots and the creation of the interior shots at a studio lot in England.

During the 19th and early 20th centuries, public speaking on diverse matters was part of the Lyceum and Chatauqua Movements. Such public speaking required style as well as some substance for edifying entertainment.

One of the earliest recorded antecedents to Freudian Analysis was Socrates' retort to the accusation by Zopyrus the Thracian that Socrates was a monster to the effect "that through the exercise of reason he [Socrates] has managed to suppress the the innate character traits that Zopyrus ascribed to him" (D'Angour, p. 152).

THE MODEL

Perhaps the ultimate question, the most fundamental question in its most general form, is "in what manner does A affect B [A > B]?" Which is different than the question on "in what manner does A become B [A >/= B]?" A becoming B is a subset of A affecting B where $A1 > A2 = B$.

Another way of looking at the nub of the problem is examining endogenous logic and exogenous actions.

An important characteristic of this model is that is is implementable in that it provides a set of neutral tools to derive solutions to personal and social problems. Although it is modestly aspirational regarding the supremacy of one's psyche, this philosophical model is in marked contrast to many alternative philosophies that are predominantly aspirational and basically do not get you to where you need to go.

Quod erat demonstrandum : which is what had to be shown; thus, it has been demonstrated.

THE THREE ELEMENTS

Power is inherently and definitionally asymmetrical. Homo politico (P) is the mind's corps of stormtroopers whose mantra is "Carpe mens!". In doing so, the animus is suppressed. Thus, the internal model is created that is exported in the form of the class structure of society.

Countervailing power does not magically appear; it can only occur if the groups seeking to balance power (whether personal, social, cultural, political, societal or national) against the hegemony of another entity have a strong sense of identity.

The behavioral phenomenon of imprinting is premised in T.

Homo rationale (R) is a component of a tri-partite mind; Ecce homo rationale is the concept that a person's whole life is rational.

PRE- AND POST-PARTUM MIND

PRE-PARTUM MIND

The term evolution applies to the genetic basis of intelligence; development applies to creation and growth of intelligence in an individual.

"Scales of Justice: an evening of live music and copyright law" presented by the Historical Society of the New York Courts on May 23, 2012, at the New York City Bar Building. You may experience the performance via its webcast which is available free to the public at the website of the Historical Society of the New York Courts.

Regarding musical tones as a medium for messages, you will be amused and instructed by reviewing the history of the Cap'n Crunch Bo'sun Whistle, and other devices, used for hijacking telephone line service. See, e.g., Ron Rosenbaum's "Secrets of the Little Blue Box" in the October, 1971, Esquire Magazine.

Alan Turing, Computing Machinery and Intelligence, Mind LIX (236) pp. 433-460 (1950).

STAGES OF PRE-CONSCIOUS DEVELOPMENT

RATE OF GROWTH OF INTELLIGENCE

BUILDING BLOCKS

Christof Koch, What is Consciousness?, Scientific American vol. 318 (#6) pp. 60-64 (June, 2018).

PATH OF MENTAL DEVELOPMENT

The speculations about the Mobius Strip model are "meta-physiological" standing in the same way to medical science as metaphysics stands in relation to physics, "meta" denoting that the discussion is beyond or outside the realm of the more comprehensible base science. Alternatively, you could classify the speculations under the rubric of science fiction.

PINPOINTS OF KNOWLEDGE THAT EXPLODE

The tri-partite mind has many antecedents preceding Freud's formulation. See, e.g., Aristotle's elements of oratory: pathos (emotion?), logos (argument?) and ethos (character or credibility?).

Preece asserts that: "In Buddhist psychology, there is no developmental model of the processes that unfold in childhood, as it assumes the development of the ego has already been established." Rob Preece, The Psychology of Buddhist Tantra p. 107 (2000, 2006). In a sense, this Buddhist belief corresponds to my concept of the "cusp of personality." Introductory Commentary, 2005 Penguin edition of The Tibetan Book of the Dead, p. xviii.

Omne trium perfectum: everything that comes in three is perfect.

W. Somerset Maugham used the term "human bondage": "The impotence of man to govern or restrain the emotions I call bondage, for a man who is under their control is not his own master...so that he is often forced to follow the worse, although he sees the better before him."

Can you slay your dragons? Can the monkey defeat the eagle? Each dragon arose in a specific point which certainly can be revisited but can that point be reformulated?

Neither the identification of the originating point nor the confrontation of that event is likely to resolve the recurring pain. What may work is the expansion of understanding through analogous events not only in your life but in other people's lives to reduce the significance of the event by expanding your theatre of understanding of the event.

PRE–PARTUM PERSONALITY

POST–PARTUM PERSONALITY

See, e.g., the life of Percy Crosby (1891-1964), a truly gifted cartoonist who was, counterintuitively, darkly cynical. He, like may other cartoonists and comics, mined the crevices of life but rather than turn to the light retreated into the dark.

P-T-R (elemental analysis) is a general model of thought, truth and policy regardless of whether it accurately depicts the biophysical processes of the mind or, alternatively, is merely a useful metaphorical fiction. Aye, that is the rub as to whether elemental analysis is subject to proof.

THE ARGUMENT

Euclid's point is what explodes into all of mathematics and physics.

Anything whether object, event, motion, etc. that can be converted into a statement can be analyzed by these rules. An act can be a statement subject to elemental analysis. A famous hypothetical regarding acts as statements was argued in Wright v. Doe d. Tatham, 112 Eng. Rep. 488

(1837). While the case itself involved the probate of a will, a hypothetical illustration was used in arguing that unsworn letters of the decedent could, as acts rather than statements, demonstrate the competency of the decedent when the will was executed. The hypothetical argument was along the line that: In the absence of a ship captain's testimony re the seaworthiness of a ship lost at sea, the fact that he took his family on the ill-fated voyage should be admitted as evidence that the captain believed the ship to be seaworthy.

Even the mundane events of everyday life are subject to analysis. See Sigmund Freud, Zur Psychopathologie des Alltagsleben (The Psychopathology of Everyday Life), 1901.

There are well known interfaces between thought and the physical world such as real estate surveys (which translate physical real estate into terms that can be referenced in written documents such as contracts and deeds) and blueprints (which translate an architect's or engineer's vision into executable instructions to a builder).

As a practice drill in P-T-R logic, one can profitably benefit over time by analyzing minor point of sale (POS) transactions in which you have participated. Elemental analysis is an approach towards broadening one's understanding with the goal of improving decision-making.

P-T-R provides a means of how to comprehend what you mean when you say you "understand."

Elemental analysis becomes more useful to you the more often you rigorously apply the model to the diverse aspects of life. Rigorous adherence to the model is essential for productive results. The non-rigorous application would simply be a mirror reflecting what you already believe.

On the very pedestrian level of ordinary everyday life, consider how you relate to money. Compare what you conclude after doing an elemental analysis with what you believe would result from a Freudian analysis. See, e.g., Freud's "Character and Anal Eroticism" (1908) in vol. 9 at pp. 169-175 of The Standard Edition of the Complete Psychological Works of Sigmund Freud.

The pain of failure, blame or guilt: Consider that failure, blame and guilt are always formulated, regardless whether internally or externally, as statements. There can be no "sense of failure", "sense of blame", or "sense of guilt" unless and until the sense is articulated (internally or externally) in the form of a statement, which, of course, is subject to elemental analysis. Now consider psychopaths who seek negative peak experiences without any sense of guilt. I suggest that the sources of their behaviors lie in extreme formulations of their cusps of personality and that they are beyond the pale of civilized society.

Some forms of analysis verge on being silly. See, e.g., Freud's interpretation of Michelangelo's statue of Moses. Sigmund Freud, Der Moses des Michelangelo (The Moses of Michelangelo) published anonymously in Imago 3 (1) pp. 15-36 (1914); an English translation appears in the SE (Standard Edition) vol. XIII.

UNIFICATION THEORY

A similar synthesis but without analytical power was suggested by Arthur Koestler in his The Ghost in the Machine (1967) and Janus: a summing up (1978). Koestler's synthesis is similar to mine with "holons" corresponding to "icons" but with "holons" having a binary (Janus) loop structure rather than the tri-partite loop structure that I believe is essential to elemental analysis.

DIRECT OBSERVATION

People living in a house together organize the space as expressions of P-T-R loops. A home can be depicted as a maze of personalities imposed on the physical structure of the house. Feng shui is a similar school of thought but seems to be more individually idiosyncratic than communal or familial.

THE TRI-PARTITE MIND

John Maynard Keynes, "Economic Possibilities for our Grandchildren" in Essays in Persuasion (London: MacMillan, 1931) 344 as noted in Sylvia Nasar, Grand Pursuit: the story of economic genius (New York: Simon & Schuster, 2011) xv.

Depicted in Kurosawa's Rashomon (1950). This cinema has been the subject of voluminous commentary, particularly noteworthy being Paul Anderer's Kurosawa's Rashomon: a vanished city, a lost brother and the voice inside his iconic films (2016). The conventional interpretation of Rashomon is that the truth of an event is developed by the perspectives and individualities of the participants and observers. At a more abstract level, Rashomon can be interpreted as the perceptions of one person whose mind encoded his perceptions of the event in a tri-partite manner.

THE PROBABILITY OF TRUTHFUL STATEMENTS

A humorous illustration of this principle is that of Mark Twain's reverse translation of The Celebrated Jumping Frog of Calaveras County (1865): "The Jumping Frog: in English, then in French, and then Clawed Back into a Civilized Language Once More by Patient, Unremunerated Toil" (1903).

"Tells" are often unreliable; there is no Pinocchio methodology to determine with certainty whether a person is speaking truth or falsehood.

"A question by itself is not evidence. It is the question with the answer that is the evIdence. For example, sometimes a question will assume something to be true. You are not, however, to conclude that an assumption in a question is true unless the answer, in your judgment, confirms that it is true. So, you must consider the question with the witness's answer, and decide whether you find the answer believable and accurate--because, again, it is the question with the answer that is the evidence." NY CJI2d Model Instructions: Preliminary Instructions: Presentation of Evidence (p. 6).

William Shakespeare, The Comedy of Errors (1594).

People lie to control the immediate encounter, in part out of convenience but also in self-recognition of an inherent weakness in their internally developed position.

Most "battles" are surface battles rather than structural battles.

Surface logic, the application of ordinary rules to the facial statements in everyday life, creates a literal interpretation (with some slight variations) of those statements. Surface logic is the home of lies (intentional misrepresentation of facts). Lies become mere statements when deconstructed with the rules of internal logic. Emotions thrive on surface logic; analysis inhabits internal logical deconstruction.

"Truth, the sum of existence" [reduced to its elements?]: John Jaques (1827-1900) wrote the poem "Oh Say, What Is Truth?" that became a hymn for The Church of Jesus Christ of Latter-Day Saints.

ALTERNATE REALITIES

The default mode for the mind is storytelling but the trick to understanding any story is to realize the alternative storylines that the mind could have chosen. Stories become encyclopedic (cumulative equivalencies [T]) reasoning that are more meaningfully understood by abstract analysis (primarily R).

Armistice Brioche

I purchased some pastries, including brioche in an escargot style, at a Starbucks. The brioche appeared to me to be small cinnamon buns, each round with a well formed spiral, abundant dark powder and no sugar frosting. At home, I enjoyed eating the brioche with it's right amount of sweetness which I attributed to the dark cinnamon powder.

A week later I returned to the same Starbucks and asked for the cinnamon brioche. The barista queried: "The chocolate brioche?" "No, they are cinnamon."" The barista pointed to the brioche on the top shelf, "You mean these?" "Yes." The barista completed my order. At home, I ate one of the brioche and tasted the cocoa powder. 11/11/2018

SEXUALITY

At the core of the the debates that occurred as Freud was developing and presenting his ideas was whether sexuality was the predominant force in forming the psyche or whether it was part of a much broader concept of being human. Much of the criticism seems to have been more of a complaint about emphasis, particularly in regards to terminology. As important as sexual forces are, I do not see any way around the concept that sexuality is but part of the gross psyche and that the gross psyche forms or molds or directs the vectors of sexual energy.

RELIGION

Elemental analysis is a general, arguably universal, model of the transformation of stimulus into meaning. A peculiar analogy exists in the death bed rituals prescribed by The Tibetan Book of the Dead regarding the time of death (life-gap-reality), reality and rebirth. Specifically, parsing of the entire set of rituals reduces the process to elements that can be reconstructed into a Western understanding of death that transcends Western traditions.

There are many complex and richly detailed tapestries (which in medieval times could function as Le Corbusier's "nomadic murals") that can be studied as encyclopedic icons. Mandalas are analogous art forms, many of which are preserved in monasteries, museums and homes but others are famously ephemeral (Tibetan sand mandalas and Southwest Native American sand mandalas). Thangkas are Buddhist icons carried by wandering story tellers that are exactly analogous to European ("Christian") medieval tapestries.

The continuum from stimulus through interpretation to meaning is known in Sanskrit as the tantra.

PHILOSOPHY AND POLICY

A major limitation of traditional market analysis as the engine of economic efficiency is externalities. Externalities are by-products of a market transaction that imposes costs and sometimes benefits to persons who did not participate in the transaction. Externalities provide a rationale for the regulation of economic activity.

John Maynard Keynes was not the exemplar embodiment of R; as a college trustee, he participated in insider trading of securities, an activity that is ultimately premised in T.

Philosophy is typically the expression of one's cusp of personality. However, to the extent that one understands in a systematic way one's own personality, philosophy can be the means to serve as a corrective lens to see life more clearly and accurately.

Your total personality is the sum of your icons organized by your cusp of personality.

As an obiter dictum and otherwise as an exceptionally fine point regarding forms of legal argument, there is a theoretical asymmetry in the proper use of Brandeis Briefs. In essence, Brandeis Briefs are proper in the support of the constitutionality of legislation but Brandeis style briefs are not proper in a formal sense to argue in court ab initio that particular legislation is unconstitutional. The distinction revolves around the power of the legislatures to legislate policy. If Congress or a state legislature already has the doctrinal power to enact specific legislation, then the argument is that the attackers need to go back to the legislature for it to re-consider the policy it propounded. This is an exceptionally fine point regarding the merry-go-round of policy and doctrine. Do not worry if you do not understand it.

THE SOCIETAL MIND

Social filters are more pronounced in minds predominantly P and T; R dominated minds are more likely to be straightforwardly honest, often to the person's social detriment.

My discussion is directed at the forms of argument; as such, it is an indirect attack on bad policy. A direct attack would be doomed to failure because the bulk of society has the mentality of Jonathan Swift's Yahoos and would repel a direct attack using the most primitive form of reasoning.

THE SOUTH PACIFIC

Samuel Clemens (Mark Twain) and Kurt Vonnegut are well known literary stylists who opposed imperialism and war. See, e.g., Kurt Vonnegut Complete Stories (2017) section 1 "War," pp. 1 - 168.

For an illustrative discussion of the politics of ethnicity, language, religion and territory, see Ramachandra Guha, India After Gandhi (2007) (in particular Chapter 9, Redrawing the Map, pp. 189-208).

Serendipitously, I received instruction in Native American law by Vine's brother Philip "Sam" Deloria when I attended the University of New Mexico School of Law.

JURY DELIBERATIONS

One of the skills necessary to be successful as a trial attorney is the ability to reformulate the client's view of the case into an argument that resonates not necessarily with the client but with the jury. Many clients adhere to kitchen table logic rather than courtroom logic. The problem with kitchen table logic is that a participant can walk away maintaining his views and proclaiming that the other person did not prove anything. But the kitchen table issue remains unresolved. In a courtroom trial, the issue will be resolved and the case needs to be tried to the jurors.

THE TEST

The One Sentence Trick: Years ago I developed a trick to force people to organize their thoughts in talking with me. I would say to a person something along the line of: "I will make a deal with you in the form of a game. I will listen to everything you have to say to me if you accept the challenge of first saying whatever you want to say but using only one sentence of ordinary length. Having done that, you would say what you said in one sentence but now expanding the one sentence to two sentences of ordinary length. Next you may use three sentences to say what you said in two sentences. You may continue the repetitious expansion until you have said everything you wanted to say." This "one sentence trick" of expansion of the base sentence rather than adding on sentences helps to quickly focus meandering conversations into actionable statements. While it might appear to be a form of elemental analysis, the trick does not utilize the P-T-R methodology. The trick is just an ordinary device to focus a conversation.

As to oracles, particularly in regard to predictive rather explanatory or normative analysis, truth in method lies in its predictive utility. If a method is not predictive, then it is just talk. In ancient Greece, persons serving as oracles sometimes spoke in riddles. Perhaps elemental analysis is just a modern riddle to intrigue a person into analyzing a problem rather than answering the question.

If you deviate from the model, any comprehensive model, not just elemental analysis, that is based in reality, you set free your demons to wreck havoc on your thoughts and actions. A comprehensive reality based model allows the better angels of our nature to emerge from our African Genesis.

Two of the most important life skills one should cultivate is the ability to listen and the understanding of human nature. Franklin Roosevelt as a young man drove about in Dutchess County and conversed with ordinary folk. As Secretary of the Navy, he hosted luncheons for politicians

visiting Washington, D. C. When ensconced at Hyde Park, he and his con-
sigliere, Louis Howe, read newspapers from around the country, which is a
form of listening. Listening, as previously noted, is a form of "looking."
Abraham Lincoln was not a policy expert prior to his presidency but he did
have a profound understanding of human nature. See, e.g., Channing Kury,
Criminal Defense and the American Character, The Suffolk Lawyer
(December, 1996) p. 11.

Q. E. D.

Q. E. D.: Quod erat demonstrandum : which is what had to be shown;
thus, it has been demonstrated.

In ancient Greek Mythology, Tantalus killed his son Pelops in an
attempt to serve him as food to Tantalus' dinner guest gods.

This passage plays off Dylan Thomas' "Do not go gentle into that
good night" (1947, 1951, 1952).

"Joy" pun: Freud.

Pax vobiscum: "Peace be with you."

IN CASE YOU WANTED TO ASK

Are the originating assumptions susceptible to P-T-R analysis? Yes.

Is P-T-R just another illusion? It is a lemma. Whether a lemma is an illusion is for you to decide for yourself. This extended essay is a heuristic device to steer the reader away from fundamental errors in thinking.

Definition of lemma: A legal fiction with talismanic qualities that uses an assumption without necessarily believing that the assumption is true but accepts the assumption's statement "as if" it were true. The mind is full of lemmas (algorithms that have no intrinsic value standing alone) other than transitioning from one proposition to another. Similar terms include catalyst, legal fiction, legal concepts other than pure legal fictions, and talismanic transformation. "As if" statements, such as legal fictions, are lemmas and are otherwise partial solutions or statements. A stepping stone to cross Heraclitus' river. Rivers are commonly used as literary devices as metaphors for life. See, e.g., Mark Twain, Life on the Mississippi (1883) and Norman Maclean, A River Runs through It (1976).

Why bother? P-T-R analysis helps to advance one's thinking to a healthier frame of mind.

Isn't this essay supposed to be about the causes of war? It is. I answered the question: "Why would fathers send their sons into a war that could not be won?" The answer lies in psychology rather than policy. Witness the conquest of the Chatham Islanders in December, 1835, by Maori warriors even though the Chatham Islanders posed no threat of any sort to the Maori people. Healthy people avoid war. Policy is not as confined as much as politicians would lead us to believe. If you accept the proposition that policy is ultimately psychology, then The Symphony of the Mind is a primer on the derivation of policy.

Is it possible for a political leader to be humanistically rational? Franklin Roosevelt was certainly so; Hitler and Tojo were delusively insane. Ho Chi Minh was relatively humanistically rational; Lyndon Johnson was not insane but was delusional and his advisors Dean Rusk (Secretary of State 1961-1969) and Robert McNamara (Secretary of Defense 1961-1968) were clueless in their analyses and policies. Rusk and McNamara both lacked commonsense. However, Johnson was rational enough in 1968 to overrule Gen. William Westmoreland's plan "Operation Fracture Jaw" to place "tactical" nuclear, as well as chemical, weapons in the theatre of war. See David B. Sanger, U.S. Commander Moved to Place Nuclear Arms in South Vietnam, NY Times, October 7, 2018, pp. 1 & 10, citing Michael Beschloss, Presidents of War (2018).

The challenge: You are welcomed to identify as many errors of fact and logic as you can find in my odyssey through the mind. Having found errors, you are invited to write your own coherent comprehensive statement of philosophy. Best of luck in that Herculean task. It might help you to remember that, whether the Blackfoot or the Ganges, "A River Runs through It."

As to all other questions, res ipsa loquitur. "The thing speaks for itself."

SWISS ARMY KNIFE

[Or, more formally, The Exegesis Lemma]

Elemental analysis is a Swiss Army knife for personal and policy analysis. Or, for a laugh, elemental analysis can be considered the Veg-O-Matic ("It slices! It dices!") of deconstruction logic.

Two of the most useful SAK tools are:

1. Every statement is composed of P-T-R elements.

2. All human behavior can be perceived as derived from personally held icons. E.g., icons are the sources for the expressions of compulsions.

There are other tools et seq. ….

APPENDIX

ELEMENTAL ANALYSIS: AN INTRODUCTORY OUTLINE

Elemental analysis is a model that progressively builds upon itself. It is the reiteration of the method that generates the increasing scale and complexity of analysis.

The basic premise is that all thought is composed of elements that obey rules of composition.

The rules of composition apply not only to the internal communication within the mind but also to the perception of external phenomena.

In other words, the rules provide the vehicle by which the imaginary universe of the mind translates the real universe of all phenomena external to the mind itself.

Each mind begins with nothing and builds an enormously complex model of itself and the universe.

To answer the question "What is the First Step?", it is helpful to first describe the simplest thoughts and then go back to the beginning.

Every thought is composed of 3 elements and only 3 elements.

These elements are real and behave by rules of existence even though they otherwise only exist in the medium of a brain serving as the physical scaffolding of the mind.

THE 3 ELEMENTS

The 3 elements are:

P which has a "greater than / lesser than" function.

T which has an "equal to" function.

R which has a readjustment or mediating function.

The P Element —

The P element corresponds with Freud's super-ego.

This Elemental Analysis reformulation of the super-ego may be referenced as an archetype denominated Homo politico.

The T Element —

The T element corresponds with Freud's id.

This Elemental Analysis reformulation of the id may be referenced as an archetype denominated Homo theatrica.

The R Element —

The R element corresponds with Freud's ego.

This Elemental Analysis reformulation of the ego may be referenced as an archetype denominated Homo rationale

PRE- AND POST-PARTUM MIND

Freud's schema (superego, id & ego) describes the psychological development of a child after the child's birth. At birth, the child's mind has by necessity developed a structure that allows it to interpret or translate perceptions. While in utero, the child's universe is defined by the mother's body and what few external events reach the fetus (e.g., sounds, pressure, medical devices).

PRE-PARTUM MIND

The creation of a child's mind begins in the physics and chemistry of the emerging brain. At some point in the early development of the fetus, an elixir of mind is present but blank. This elixir has the special characteristic of translating perception into an abstract structure that is readable by the child's brain.

THE ELIXIR

The elixir is an electro-chemical soup. This soup has the characteristic of receiving an initial perception and then organizing its structure into any of three alternative forms. There may be some law of physics as to the nature of matter itself that comes into play.

THE ELIXIR'S CHOICE

Until the first stimulus, the elixir can not think and is otherwise incapable of processing information. Its composition is such that an electro-chemical code can be created out of building blocks that by themselves can not function to process information. The initial stimulus forces the elixir to choose to organize itself.

BUILDING BLOCKS

P   a greater than / lesser than function that is directional (can go in either of two directions but not both directions in any one bit of code).

T   an equal function that goes in both directions simultaneously.

R   a compiler function that measures and mediates the strength of the P and T functions.

ELECTRONIC ENGINEERING

Every one of these concepts are ordinary and well within the ken of millions of engineers who can build numerous devices based on these concepts. But not a single one of those devices will have a psyche, cognition beyond computation. Where is the magical transformation?

IMPORTANCE OF ELECTRONIC ENGINEERING MODEL

The electronic engineering model is important as the key to the internalization of an outside stimulus. The stimulus itself is not incorporated into the elixir. The elixir converts the disturbance into a P or T function in the electro-chemical soup.

THE ELIXIR TRANSFORMED

Once the soup is organized into its most rudimentary structure, it is no longer soup but is now a proto-mind. The rules by which the proto-mind developes are no longer electronic engineering rules. The developmental rules exist and are testable.

PATH OF MENTAL DEVELOPMENT

Elixir micro-drop

Neural tube

Segmented brain

PRE-PARTUM PERSONALITY

The pre-partum personality is determined by the P, T & R structure of the fetus' mind. By the time of birth, the mind has already become a Gordian Knot of circuits in which there are preferred paths. The preference one path over other paths is what gives the child its initial personality. That initial psyche is the infant's set of mental tools with which to explore life.

POST-PARTUM PERSONALITY

The initial birth personality is molded thereafter by interacting with the external world. Freudian factors progressively advance through childhood until puberty and adolescence. Thereafter, the psyche deals with life with what tools it has at hand.

THE RULES

Every thought is a Mobius strip loop composed of varying combinations of P, T & R. Every component of a loop is also a Mobius strip loop itself.

REGRESSION

By disentangling the loops, one can discover the original organizing impulse structure. Thus solving the Gordian Knot riddle.

THE TEST

Elemental analysis, being a universal (and not a partial) philosophy, is subject to a myriad of tests, whether by logicians, psychiatrists, medical researchers investigating human ontogeny, etc. Each investigator will reach his own conclusion that may refute or confirm a part of elemental analysis. The test, in the end, is not whether I have or can prove the truth of every component of this theory. The test is whether you in your own way can implement these ideas into meaningful beliefs and actions.

REALITY

If elemental analysis is a description of reality, how can reality be measured to test whether elemental analysis corresponds with reality? A model must first be created that within itself has characteristics, that if true, can be observed in reality.

MEASUREMENT

To compare the model with reality requires measurement. Measurement requires mathematics. Initially, at least, all that is needed is Euclidean inspiration and rudimentary mathematical calculation.

THE ASSUMPTION

Assume that a thought is a structure that is ultimately constructed from three, and just three, types of building blocks. That each building block is composed of these same type of three building blocks. That the building blocks interact to create a structure that is an implementable thought.

IMPLEMENTABLE THOUGHT

An implementable thought is a thought that can create further thoughts or bodily action. Ab initio there must be a critical size to the structure at which the internal logic interprets stimuli.

THE NON-FUNCTIONING MODEL

The non-functioning model is the most primitive conception of how thought is structured but is insufficient to describe how thought works.

FUNCTIONING MODEL

To communicate within itself, the structure must have a loop function. The loop function is fundamental to creating a functioning mental structure. The postulate is that each element (P, T & R) is a loop.

THE LOOP STRUCTURE

As each element attaches to another element, each element can refer back to the other with information from another part of that element's loop.

MOBIUS STRIP CONJECTURE

Each loop is a Mobius Strip. The Mobius Strip Conjecture postulates that thought is composed of interlinked rotating Mobius Strips, the size (particularly the length) of which and the speed of rotation determine the time it takes to fix a thought [which is known to be about one-tenth of a second]. If you can accept the conjecture, then the carousel-Ferris wheel phenomenon of the mind is explicable and progressive thought is explained. Q. E. D.

BIBLIOGRAPHY

Stella Adler, Stella Adler on America's Master Playwrights (Alfred A. Knopf, New York, 2012).

Paul Anderer, Kurosawa's Rashomon: a vanished city, a lost brother, and the voice inside his iconic films (2016).

Robert Ardrey, African Genesis (1961); The Territorial Imperative (1966); The Social Contract (1970); The Hunting Hypothesis (1976).

Daren Aronofsky, Pi (cinema, 1998).

Marcus Aurelius, Meditations (written from about 161 A.D. to 180 A.D.); George Long translation (1862); Dover Thrift Edition (1997).

An antecedent of the cusp of personality is Marcus Aurelius' daimon (soul of man; the deity that is planted in you), preservation of which he argues is essential for a good life. Marcus Aurelius suggests that philosophy is the only guide to such a good life and in doing so, although Emperor of the Roman Empire, silently eschews power as the guide. Herein lies a key to understanding the nature of power. Towards the beginning of Book VIII, Aurelius states: "If then you have truly seen where the matter lies, throw away the thought of how you might seem to others, and be content if you live the rest of your life in the manner that your nature wills." I find it paradoxical that an emperor should be so outspoken in favor of individuality. If you doubt the paradox, go further to read Aurelius' rhetorical question: "Alexander and Gaius and Pompeius, what are they in comparison with Diogenes and Heraclitus and Socrates?"

As an obiter dictum, reading or reciting Meditations is similar to the reading or reciting Zen texts such as The Tibetan Book of the Dead. Many passages in Meditations are koans, statements designed to elicit thought rather than to state truth. Marcus Aurelius counsels, much like a Zen master, an indifference towards death. Marcus Aurelius was one of the first modern men whose decisions, actions and writings are historically accessible and who made rational decisions in the face of complex issues of politics, foreign relations and finance. He was much more sophisticated than Julius Caesar and his cohort of elite Romans.

Nina Avramova, CNN article (09/26/2018) "Mediterranean Diet Could Prevent Depression."

L. Frank Baum, The Wizard of Oz (cinema, 1939) which was based on the book The Wonderful Wizard of Oz (1900) and perhaps other books in the series.

Michael Beschloss, Presidents of War (2018).

Boethius, The Consolation of Philosophy (V. E. Watts translation 1969, 1998) written in 523-524. Worth reading as an exercise in testing one's own understanding of philosophy against a counterpoint written by a sophisticated man who participated in practical politics.

Carl T. Bogus, The Hidden History of the Second Amendment, U.C. Davis Law Review, vol. 31, no. 2 (1998) p. 309 et seq.

Josef Breuer and Sigmund Freud, Studies on Hysteria [Studien über Hysterie] (1895).

Jacob Bronowski, Science and Human Values (1956).

William Jennings Bryan, "Cross of Gold" speech at the Democratic National Convention in Chicago, July 9,1896, as well as many other places and dates.

C. R. Carpenter, "Behavior and Social Relations of the Howling Monkey, " Comparative Psychology Monographs, John Hopkins University (May, 1934).

Lewis Carroll, Alice's Adventures in Wonderland (1865).

Abram Chayes, Thomas Ehrlich & Andreas Lowenfeld, International Legal Process: materials for an introductory course vol. I & II (Little, Brown & Co., 1968).

Henri Charpentier, The Henri Charpentier Cookbook (1945, 1970).

Winston S. Churchill, Step by Step: political writings — 1936-1939 (1939).

Graham Coleman, an editor of The Tibetan Book of the Dead (The Great Liberation by Hearing in the Intermediate States) 2005 Penguin edition of The Tibetan Book of the Dead, p. xxxiv.

Carlo Collodi, The Adventures of Pinocchio (1883).

Joseph Conrad, The Heart of Darkness (1899, 1902).

Frederick Crews, Freud: the making of an illusion (2017); reviewed by Lisa Appignanesi, "Freud's Clay Feet," The New York Review of Books Oct. 26, 2017.

Armand D'Angour, Socrates in Love: the making of a philosopher (Bloomsbury Publishing, 2019).

Bryony Davies, Sigmund Freud's Collection: highlights from the Freud Museum London (Freud Museum London, 2019).

Vine Deloria, Jr., Custer Died for Your Sins (1969); We Talk, You Listen (1970).

Jared Diamond, Guns, Germs and Steel (1997).

Charles Dickens, Bleak House (1852-53) was a satire of the British judicial system and was based in part on the litigation of Wright v. Doe d. Tatham, 112 Eng. Rep. 488 (1837).

Ronald L. DiSanto and Thomas J. Steele, Guidebook to Zen and the Art of Motorcycle Maintenance (1990).

Tadeusz Dolega-Mostowicz, Kariera Nikodema Dyzmy (1932).

F. W. Dyson, A. S. Eddington and C. Davidson, A determination of the deflection of light by the Sun's gravitational field, from observations made at the total eclipse of 29 May 1919," Philosophical Transactions of the Royal Society 220A: 291-333 (1920).

Otto Eckstein, Water Resource Development: the economics of project evaluation (1958).

Bernard B. Fall, Street Without Joy: the French debacle in Indochina (1961, 1963, 1964, 1994).

Essential reading for understanding the prelude to the United States injecting itself into the Viet Nam conflict. An important case report for any comprehensive course in policy studies.

If "insanity is doing the same thing over again and expecting a different result", then the United States' excursion into Viet Nam was an insane act. Simply compare the history of the previous French excursion's strategy and tactics with the subsequent American strategy and tactics. Not a dime's worth of difference but it cost 58,000 American lives to learn what was already known. An eerie coincidence is that about 55,000 French were previously killed in the First Viet Nam War. [Anne Swardson, "France's Lonely Vietnam Memorial", Washington Post, February 24, 1997: "About 55,000 French troops and civilians were killed in the fighting in Indochina...."] I have no clue what significance, if any, there is in this coincidence. Bear in mind that estimates of causalities vary widely. Fall lists the figure of 75,867 French killed in Indochina during 1946-54 [Street Without Joy, Appendix II]. There are other estimates as well. The model that best explains the American excursion into Viet Nam is psychology, perhaps social psychology, rather than one of "the national interest", international diplomacy in the Cold War, economics or any of the other models that might be trotted out in discussing the war. These partial models, these fictions, are merely red herrings that distract one's focus from the cusp of decision making by which leaders and fathers ultimately chose war and sacrifice over peace and growth.

Frances Fitzgerald, Fire in the Lake (1972).

John Fowles, The Aristos: a self-portrait of ideas (1964).

Sigmund Freud, The Complete Psychological Works of Sigmund Freud (Standard Edition), 24 vols. (W. W. Norton, New York, 1989).

Mohandas K. Gandhi, Gandhi's Autobiography: the story of my experiments with truth (1948); part IV, section XLIV "Some Reminiscences of the Bar" discusses the practice of law as a liar's profession.

Genesis: 22.

Peter Gay (ed.), The Freud Reader, (W. W. Norton, New York, 1976).

Jeffrey Gettleman & Suhasini Raj, "Caste Is Still Enforced in a Changing India, With Fists and Blades," The New York Times CLXVIII (no. 58,150) p.8 (Sunday, Nov. 18, 2018) reports an act of scalping to enforce the caste hierarchy in That, India, in September, 2018.

Gilbert & Sullivan, H.M.S. Pinafore, in particular "When I Was a Lad" in Act I (1878).

Kurt Godel, "Uber formal unentschiedeneidbare Sätze der Principia Mathematica und verwandter Systeme, I", Monatshefte fur Mathematik und Physik, 38(1): 173-198 (1931).

Ramachandra Guha, India After Gandhi (2007) (in particular Chapter 9, Redrawing the Map, pp. 189-208).

George Frideric Handel, Messiah (1741).

Roy Heath, The Reasonable Adventurer (1964).

Ernest Hemingway, For Whom the Bell Tolls (1940).

Herman Hesse, Das Glasperlenspiel (1943).

Damien Hirst, Treasures from the Wreck of the Unbelievable (cinema, 2017).

Stephen Johnson, How Shostakovich Changed My Mind (Notting Hill Editions, 2019).

Jumanji (cinema, 1995): a comedic depiction of the mind.

Joseph B. Kadane and David A. Schum, A Probabilistic Analysis of the Sacco and Vanzetti Evidence (1996).

Stanley Karnow, Vietnam: a history (1983).

Kautilya, Arthashastra (The Science of Politics), two millennia ago.

John Maynard Keynes, The Economic Consequences of the Peace (1919); "Economic Possibilities for our Grandchildren" in Essays in Persuasion (London: MacMillan, 1931) 344 as noted in Sylvia Nasar, Grand Pursuit: the story of economic genius (New York: Simon & Schuster, 2011) xv.

Winston L. King, Zen and the Way of the Sword: arming the samurai psyche (1993).

Rudyard Kipling, The Ballad of East and West, 1889; At the Pit's Mouth (1888) re Tertium Quid; Epitaphs of the War (1914-18).

Christof Koch, What is Consciousness?, Scientific American vol. 318 (#6) pp. 60-64 (June, 2018).

Arthur Koestler, The Ghost in the Machine (1967); Janus: a summing up (1978).

Koran 37:100-113.

Jerzy Kosinski, Being There (1970).

Akira Kurosawa, Rashomon (cinema, 1950). The conventional interpretation of Rashomon is that the truth of an event is developed by the perspectives and individualities of the participants and observers. At a more abstract level, Rashomon can be interpreted as the perceptions of one person whose mind encoded his perceptions of the event in a tri-partite manner.

Channing Kury, Criminal Defense and the American Character, The Suffolk Lawyer (Dec., 1996) p.11; Prolegomena to Conservation: a fisheye review, Natural Resources Journal 17 (3): pp. 493-509 (1977); Reader's Guide to "Peace with God the Creator, Peace with All of Creation", Natural Resources Journal 30 (1): pp. 9-11 (1990); correspondence to Wendell Kury (March 23, 2010) re Wolf's bridge between physics and consciousness.

Gloria Kury, The Early Work of Luca Signorelli: 1465 - 1490 (Garland Publishing, New York & London, 1978), Preface to the Garland Edition.

Daniel Lang, Casualties of War, The New Yorker (October 18, 1969).

Jean Larteguy, The Centurions (1960, 1961); The Praetorians (1961, 1963). These two books explore in many ways the psyches of soldiers in combat. Bear in mind that while many statements are unsound they are nonetheless representative of the forces shaping a soldier's thinking. The Centurions {pp. 504-512} is sometimes mentioned as a source for the explication of the justification of torture as in a time-bomb scenario.

Camille Lassale, G. David Batty, Amaria Baghdadli, Felice Jacka, Almudena Sanchez-Villegas, Mika Kivimaki & Tasnime Akbaraly, "Healthy dietary indices and risk of depressive outcomes: a systematic review and meta-analysis of observational studies," Molecular Psychiatry (2018).

Martin E. Latz, Gain the Edge: negotiation strategies for lawyers (December 12, 2017, at Melville, New York) under the sponsorship of the New York State Bar Association.

D. H. Lawrence, Women in Love (1920).

Aldo Leopold, A Sand County Almanac (1949).

Jimmy LeSage, Forty Years of Authentic Wellness (2017).

Michael Lewis, The Big Short (2010).

Abraham Lincoln, First Inaugural Address (March 4, 1861).

Robert M. Lindner, The Fifty-Minute Hour (1955); Must You Conform? (1956) [which contains chapters discussing: "The Mutiny of the Young", "Homosexuality and the Contemporary Scene", "Political Creed and Character", "The Instinct of Rebellion", "Must You Conform?", & "Education for Maturity"].

Gene Lyons, Psychology's theories Don't Always Stand the Test of Time, The Progressive Populist vol. 25 (#3) p. 7 (February 15, 2019).

Norman Maclean, A River Runs through It (1976).

Niccoló Machiavelli, Il Principe [The Prince] (1532).

Marshall McLuhan, Understanding Media: the extensions of man (1964): "The medium is the message."

Norman Mailer, The Armies of the Night: the novel as history / history as a novel (1968).

Abraham Maslow, Toward a Psychology of Being (1962, 1968).

Stanley Milgram, "Behavioral Study of Obedience," Journal of Abnormal and Social Psychology 67 (4): 371-378 (1963).

Claude Monet, Water Lilies (series of paintings; early Twentieth Century).

Alan Moore, Batman: The Killing Joke (DC Comics, 1988). The Joker: "If I'm going to have a past, I prefer it to be multiple choice." [p. 46 of 2019 deluxe edition]

John K. Noyes, The Mastery of Submission: inventions of masochism (1997). A tour de force exploration of the psyche observed through the lens of sado-masochism. Chapter 5 (pp. 140-163) focuses in detail on Freudian theory. Noyes teases out the thread of sado-masochism to unravel the Gordian Knot of the entire psyche.

Ohashi, Reading the Body (1991).

M. B. Parten, "Social Participation among Preschool Children," J. of Abnormal and Social Psychology 27 (3): 243-269 (1932); "Social Play among Preschool Children," J. of Abnormal and Social Psychology 28 (2): 136-147 (1933).

The Pentagon Papers (available in many forms of publication).

Robert M. Pirsig, Zen and the Art of Motorcycle Maintenance: an inquiry into values (1974).

Plato, Republic (about 380 B.C.)

Plato: complete works (Cooper & Hutchinson [eds.], Hackett Publishing, 1997).

Robert Pollack, The Missing Moment: how the unconscious shapes modern science (1999).

The "missing moment" time lapse in cognition seems to be the neu-rophysiological basis for requiring motorists to come to a complete stop at stop signs and red lights. The geography of such traffic controlled intersec-tions is such that the motorist can not scan sufficiently in rolling through the traffic control to perceive another vehicle or object moving into the intersection from just beyond the tight horizons of the intersection. The time lapse is directly applicable to umpire and referee calls in sport events, as is suggested by the umpire joke in the Second Preface, supra.

Rob Preece, The Psychology of Buddhist Tantra (2000, 2006).

Marcel Proust, Swann's Way (also known as: Remembrance of Things Past), 1913.

Pushpesh Pant, India Cookbook (2010).

Charles Randolph and Adam McKay, The Big Short screenplay (based upon the book by Michael Lewis) (Buff Revised, May 11, 2015).

Ron Rosenbaum, Secrets of the Little Blue Box, Esquire Magazine (Oct., 1971).

Jeremy D. Safran (editor), Psychoanalysis and Buddhism: an unfold-ing dialogue (2003).

David B. Sanger, U.S. Commander Moved to Place Nuclear Arms in South Vietnam, NY Times, October 7, 2018, pp. 1 &10.

S. van Schaik, Tibetan Zen: discovering a lost tradition pp. 124, 135-136 (2015).

Erwin Schrodinger, "Die gegenwartige Situation in der Quanten-mechanik", Naturwissenschaften 23(48): 807-812 (1935).

Scientific American [Special Issue: Truth, Lies and Uncertainty], vol. 321, no. 3 (September, 2019).

"John Thomas Scopes and William Jennings Bryan. The World's Most Famous Court Trial: Tennessee Evolution Case: A Complete Steno-graphic Report of the Famous Court Test", National Book Co. (Cincinnati, ca. 1925).

Rod Serling, The Twilight Zone (television series, 1959-1964).

William Shakespeare, The Comedy of Errors, 1594; Hamlet (Act III, Scene 1) 1603, 1604, 1623; Henry the Fourth, Part 1 (Act 3, Scene 1) 1598; Titus Andronicus, 1594; The Tragedy of Macbeth (Act 1, Scene 1), 1623.

Adam Smith, The Wealth of Nations (1776).

Ronald P. Sokol, Justice after Darwin (The Michie Co., Charlottesville, 1975). See pp. 52-53 regarding Prof. F. D. G. Riddle's use of the umpire joke to illustrate three different theories of law.

Ro Spankie, Sigmund Freud's Desk: an anecdotal guide (Freud Museum London, 2015).

I. F. "Izzy" Stone, I. F. Stone's Weekly, 1953-1971.

Galen Strawson, Things That Bother Me: death, freedom, the self, etc. (2018).

William Strunk & E. B. White, The Elements of Style (1959; there are several prior and later versions; I was instructed as a college freshman in an English composition course that relied on the 1959 edition).

D.T. Suzuki, Introduction to Zen Buddhism (1934).

Jonathan Swift, Gulliver's Travels (1726).

Dylan Thomas, "Do not go gentle into that good night" (1947, 1951, 1952).

David Thoreau, Resistance to Civil Government (a/k/a On the Duty of Civil Disobedience) (1849).

The Tibetan Book of the Dead, 2005 Penguin edition.

Robert Traver (John Voelker), Anatomy of a Murder (1958).

Alan Turing, Computing Machinery and Intelligence, Mind LIX (236) pp. 433-460 (1950).

Ivan Turgenev, Fathers and Sons (1862).

Mark Twain, The Chronicle of Young Satan (1897-1900); Life on the Mississippi (1883).

Vietnam as the Past, Summer 1983 issue of The Wilson Quarterly (vol. VII, #3, pp. 94-139).

Kurt Vonnegut, Complete Stories (2017) section 1 "War," pp. 1 - 168.

Peter T. White and Winfield Parks, Behind the Headlines in Viet Nam, National Geographic (vol. 131, # 2, pp. 149-193) published in February, 1967.

John Henry Wigmore, A Treatise on the System of Evidence in Trials at Common Law (1904);

The Problem of Proof. Illinois Law Review 8: 77 (1913); The Science of Judicial Proof as Given by Logic, Psychology and General Experience and Illustrated in Judicial Trials, Boston: Little, Brown and Co. (1913); The Science of Judicial Proof as Given by Logic, Psychology and General Experience and Illustrated in Judicial Trials (second edition), Boston: Little, Brown and Co. (1931); The Science of Judicial Proof as Given by Logic, Psychology and General Experience and Illustrated in Judicial Trials (third edition), Boston: Little, Brown and Co. (1937).

Ludwig Wittgenstein, Tractatus Logico-Philosophicus (1921).

Fred Alan Wolf, Taking the Quantum Leap: the new physics for non-scientists (1981, 1989).

W. B. Yeats, The Second Coming (1919).

Eli Zaretsky, Secrets of the Soul: a social and cultural history of psychoanalysis (2004).

The Zero Theorem (cinema, 2013).

THE AUTHOR

CHANNING KURY practices philosophy in the guise of law on Long Island, New York. He attended The Mercersburg Academy, Cornell University and the University of New Mexico School of Law. He is a member of the state bars of New York and California.

Channing Kury is the author of professional articles on avian biology, natural resource management, conservation philosophy and Abraham Lincoln's last jury trial. He also edited Enclosing the Environment: NEPA's transformation of conservation into environmentalism (1985).

He has practiced law for over forty years. In his masterpiece trial, he gained the acquittal of his client by asserting an entrapment defense in Operation Panama that was prosecuted by the United States Attorney for New Mexico.

ChanningKury@ptrpolicyanalysis.com